Creating Effective & Successful Teams

Creating Effective & Successful Teams

Thomas R. Keen, Ph.D.

ICHOR BUSINESS BOOKS

An imprint of

Purdue University Press

West Lafayette, Indiana

*To my wife, who has been my lifelong
friend and inspiration, and to TJ
and Cherie, who have taught me how
to be a good father.*

10 9 8 7 6 5 4 3 2 1

Printed in the United States of America

Library of Congress Cataloging-in-Publication Data

Keen, Thomas R.
    Creating effective & successful teams / Thomas R. Keen.
        p. cm.
    Includes bibliographical references and index.
    ISBN 1-55753-289-3 (alk. paper)
    1. Teams in the workplace.   I. Title: Creating effective and successful teams.   II. Title.

    HD66.K396   2003
    658.4′02—dc21

                                                                                    2002036800

Contents

List of Practical Tips

Chapter 1
Why Teams?

Teams Have Been Used Successfully for Decades

Teams have been around in many types, in many countries, for many decades. Teams have become part of the major changes that are occurring in American business. In the early 1960s, workers began to input into the operational aspect of companies. They were organized into small groups in the 1970s to identify how manufacturing processes could be made more efficient.

As the impact of downsizing and rightsizing began to occur in the mid-1980s, companies still required the same amount of work to be done, but with less people. Companies found themselves in a new work environment. The days of high profits that followed World War II allowed departments to mushroom in size. In the early 1980s, these departments became the targets for cost reduction measures as the ability to raise prices to stabilize profits was no longer available. Managers had to find cost-effective ways to get the work done without raising prices. Taking groups of people from various departments to solve a problem or complete a task seemed to be a good solution when increasing headcount was not an option. A benefit to this staffing solution began to surface in the early 1990s. More and more companies began to use teams as they determined that teams were a strong way to approach a situation that had multiple dimensions. Teams of people with multiple skill sets, experience levels, and technical competencies outperformed individuals acting alone trying to solve the problem or complete the task.

Teams in the Twenty-First Century

As the twenty-first century begins, companies are much different in configuration. They have fewer levels of hierarchy and have fewer internal resources to operate effectively. In addition, the explosion of technological advances has resulted in managers having more information faster and with less time to analyze it. Add to that the new global marketplace, and it becomes obvious that new and better ways of operating had to be found.

As a result, it would appear that teams are being utilized extensively and are now here to stay as part of the new business landscape and new service economy. That is because teams are more flexible than old hierarchical, bureaucratical companies. The traditional organizational structures have proven to be too cumbersome and slow to move in this new business economy. The quick start-up companies of the e-revolution have impacted significantly the way old-economy organizations work. Cross-functional teams, the team matrix system, and a team-based organizational structure fit into that need for adaptability and speed in this new business environment.

Therefore, in order to stay competitive in this global economy, businesses must continue to reduce costs, improve quality, and increase production. Many companies, such as IBM, Honeywell, and Volvo have found that teamwork helps accomplish these strategies. Many other large and small companies have successfully used teams to solve problems, improve efficiency, and encourage innovation. Teams have also been proven to provide a much-needed tool for better relationships between management and unions, distributors, and suppliers. In a recent study by Gregory (1999), teams were recognized as a suitable strategy for improving an organization's performance among approximately 9 out of 10 of the companies who responded.

What Is a Team?

Before deciding how to use teams effectively, a definition of the word *team* seems appropriate. *The American Heritage Dictionary* defines *team* as, "A group organized to work together or a group on the same side—as in a game." When one thinks of a team, usually it relates to sports—such as baseball, football, or basketball—but the word *team* is also related now to business. In terms of a business orientation a team is assembling employees into groups with a common aim and a need to work as a unit to achieve a desired result. In many ways a business team is not much different from a sports team. All team members are working together on a stated objective, such as solving a company problem.

Belbin (2000), considered to be the Father of Teams for his work in team dynamics, states that groups are different from teams. A group consists of people brought together for a common purpose. In groups, as the number of people increases, the identity of each member diminishes. Belbin states that the larger the number, the greater the chance to have a "group identity and herd instinct to take over." Once that happens, the group tends to follow the "pack leader", such as in mass rallies. A very different dynamic occurs on teams. According to Belbin, a team consists of a limited number of people who are selected and assembled with a shared objective to accomplish. Each member tries to find a "personal identity" within that team setting. So, the key difference between groups and teams is in the dynamics and objective of the reason why the people are brought together.

Peter Drucker (Verespej, 1998) best summarized the impact of teams as being analogous to the wonderful music created by a symphony orchestra that far exceeds the individual talents of each musician. Teams are known to streamline functions faster; be more flexible in changing products and responding to customer needs; drive up quality; and result in greater customer satisfaction. Teams also have another advantage in this age of outsourcing as a strategy. Internally built teams can also be disbanded once their activity is completed. A large pharmaceutical company uses teams very effectively as an alternative strategy to outsourcing. In this company, an employee can identify an initiative that has short-term, long-term, or cost-saving implications to it. Once approved by local management, the person can then go through the organization to identify the *right* people they need to accomplish the task. What is important, however, is that once the task is complete, all members return to their original assignments and locations. So far it has proven to be an effective strategy to create customer satisfaction. The fact that the teams can be assembled so easily, work together so well, and accept disbandment is a testament on how to utilize teams effectively.

Different Types of Teams

Teams can be in many configurations and sizes and are called various names. However, according to Dumaine (1994), there are five basic types of teams:

1. Work Teams.   These teams are permanent and do the day-to-day work of the organization. If empowered to make decisions about how the work is done, they are called *self-managed* or *high-performance teams*. Used by two-thirds of the companies in a recent survey, work teams are becoming more popular.

2. Problem-Solving Teams.   This kind of team is the most popular type in U.S. business. A recent survey found that 91 percent of the companies use this type of team, up from about 60 percent seven years ago. These teams are comprised of workers who come together to solve a particular problem and disband thereafter.

3. Management Teams.   This kind of team is comprised of managers from the business' different functions, such as manufacturing and sales, and its members coordinate the work among other teams.

4. Virtual Teams.   This new type of work team has a constantly changing membership as the team's needs for different skills change. Members also take their turns as team leader.

5. Quality Circles.   These teams are used by 65 percent of the companies that responded to a recent survey (Dumaine 1994). Many believe this type of team is on its way out because it focuses on solving minor quality problems but is not involved in making major changes in how the work is done. Therefore, quality circles' performance gains are usually small.

Another interesting explanation of the different types of teams is offered by Katzenbach and Smith (1993). They theorized that teams might be identified differently based on their evolution to what they call *high-performance teams*. These groups include working groups, pseudo-teams, potential teams, real teams, and high-performance teams. Groups that are brought together with no significant incremental performance need or opportunity are called *working groups.* Working groups primarily are assembled to share information, best practices, or other data that results in a shared improvement of responsibilities.

The next level is *pseudo-teams.* These groups are brought together without a common purpose or set of desired outcomes. These are the weakest of all groups and are not really productive. Another group, *potential teams,* focus on producing a result that has a significant performance impact on the organization. However, potential teams lack accountability. When accountability is added to a group, then a "real" team is formed. A *real team* is a group that is equally committed to a common purpose, goals, or results.

The last great type of team is a *high-performance team.* These teams have members who are deeply committed to one another's professional growth and success. The high-performance team significantly outperforms all other types of teams. Regardless of the name assigned to the group, these five descriptions might mistakenly be called *teams* in some operations.

What Are the Basic Components of Teams?

There are four fundamental components of teams: output, interdependence, commitment, and accountability. The members must have common objectives, a reason to interface with each other, and a defined outcome toward which the team can direct its efforts. There are usually interdependent working relationships that are created, enhanced, or otherwise solidified by working in teams. Each team member must be committed to the group's effort, and, more importantly, believe in the importance of its objectives or goals and have ownership of its desired outcome. A team must have members who share common goals and an overall principle of purpose to provide meaning to their work. Individual team members should understand that each member depends on the other to complete their assignments, but have specific assignments for which they are responsible. Any lack of dedication to the overall team effort is a recipe for disaster and will ultimately reduce the team's effectiveness. Finally, any team, whether it is a business unit, department, or division, must maintain the sponsorship and have the confidence of the organization of which it is part. In order to be effective, any team must be held responsible, as a group, by a higher level within the organization. Renegade teams or teams without a purpose and a reporting relationship to a higher level will usually be unproductive.

One objective of some teams is to exercise control over and to create some sort of change. An example of such an objective is using teams to change the way decisions are made within the organization. Ideally, a team should act independently to make decisions and create changes. It is sometimes very difficult for organizations to adjust and accept this approach of empowering groups, not specific managers, to solve problems and make decisions. However, the benefit to the organization may well be increased efficiency of individual members, as well as the ability to affect change within the organization. Possibly of greater importance to the organization is that employees will learn how to control change on a self-directed basis versus having change directed from higher management or from external forces.

Benefits of Team Building

Today, leaders and managers are faced with new challenges in this rapidly changing business environment driven by quantum technology changes; unstable markets driving short-term decision making; massive mergers and acquisitions; customer sophistication; and employee turnover and restlessness. Organizations must build new structures and employees must master new skill sets in order to compete and survive effectively.

As work settings become more complex and involve increased numbers of interpersonal interactions, individual effort has less impact on companies. In order to increase efficiency and effectiveness, a group effort is required. To fill that void, teams have become a primary organizational structure strategy. Utilization of the team concept is a critical building block to improve an organization's overall effectiveness and must be considered as an integral element of organizational change.

Broadscale utilization of teams can advance the value of employees in many organizations by focusing on any of the following four team principles: setting goals and priorities, deciding on means and methods, understanding the way in which teams work, and examining the quality of employee interrelationships. To be effective, a team needs to begin with the awareness or perception of a problem and be followed sequentially by data collection, data sharing, analysis of the problem, evaluation of viable alternatives, and development of a clear-cut action plan. The ideal but not always practical goal is to have the teams involved with the inception, implementation, and evaluation of their plans. This sequence can be repeated each time new problems are identified.

Teams Can Also Have Some Downsides

A. T. Kearny, a major U.S. management consulting firm, estimated that nine out of ten teams fail. That may because a team is not only a number of employees, but also a group that is associated in some joint action for the organization. Successful teamwork is the cooperative or coordinated effort of a group of people acting together as a team toward a common cause that benefits the organization and team members.

However, there are also some downsides to teams. Group decision making takes time and attention away from an individual's primary responsibilities and tasks. In addition, the time away from the office and the time needed to make teams work effectively can be a serious drawback when speed is required. Making a decision usually takes a group longer than an individual.

Another downside is that the group mentality might promote the "let the other person do it" and the "just along for a free ride" attitudes of some team members. Because everyone is responsible for the task, no one feels individually responsible. If the team fails, there will be others to blame. Group members disagree, bicker, argue, and in other ways conflict with one another. Their dependence on each other means that at times they will have conflicts. Conflict can tear relationships apart, delay serious work, and even prevent completion of a project.

In addition, groups are also criticized because they can go astray and can come up with wild, impractical proposals. Finally, groups can undermine authority. If workers are put into teams, their cohesiveness can make them better able to resist management direction.

Working together demands constant and careful attention to making a team operate effectively. Teamwork is a beneficial productivity strategy in two ways. It not only gets the job done, but it also helps employees learn from their experiences, develop their competence, and be more productive in the future (Caudron, 1994).

There also may be significant resistance to using teams, which spawns a built-in, self-fulfilling prophecy of failure when the team system is instituted. According to Katzenbach and Smith (1993), there are three main factors that cause organizational resistance to teams. First, there maybe a lack of conviction among employees, or even management, that teams will work to solve problems and enhance productivity. This lack of conviction might be due to a general misconception that teams hinder work, productivity, and decisive action or due to a lack of performance-driven purpose for teams. This lack of performance-driven purpose can cause failure by not providing the team with specific, achievable objectives up-front that can be accomplished with the collaborative effort of a team.

The second factor is the personal discomfort and risk associated with employees being on teams. Many people fear or do not like working on teams. Teams can also represent to the individual not only an additional burden on their workload, but also a risk to their personal accomplishments or career advancement.

Thirdly, weak organizational performance ethics may also be a factor to team resistance. The reluctance of team members to link one's career to a team activity may generate significant resistance. Also, lack of management commitment to hold employees, or themselves for that matter, accountable as an organizational shortfall is a distinct problem that hinders team effectiveness.

To avoid these pitfalls, the road to a successful team is paved with a certain code of conduct that should be followed. Each team member should be present and punctual to meetings. When a team member is absent, the team misses his or her input. If the team makes decisions with which the absent member disagrees, there could be a problem.

Each team member should listen to the ideas of the other members and respect what was said. A lack of respect could also cause problems within the group or the agenda.

Each team member should have a win-win attitude. Team members should strive to make all decisions in a way that involves everyone, which produces a winning situation. Being positive can also help when trying to approach new ideas or when implementing recommendations.

The team should stay on target and be focused. A team may often lose the focus of the topic being discussed. It helps to maintain a team calendar of each individual event and to update it as the team progresses. Also, it is necessary to make sure that each member of the team has a copy of the calendar or agenda; thus, everyone has an idea about what needs to be accomplished at each meeting.

So, Are Teams the Only Solution to Evaluate?

Are teams the only solution to problem solving? Absolutely not. In the twenty-first century, organizations will have to be agile and quick to respond to the new competitive landscape. Some organizations buy rather than invent a solution. For example, reflect on all the mergers and acquisitions occurring in most industries. Organizations can hire external consultants to develop solutions, but how much time is expended to brief and manage the consultant? An organization can try an organic solution by using an internal consultant, but the same problem exists. Teams are not always the only way or, quite frankly, the correct way in some cases to solve a problem.

But . . . Teams Are Everywhere

Teams might not be the only solution, but in today's fast-paced, slimmer business organizations, teams are gaining popularity. In business, there are product teams, quality teams, and project teams. Engleberg and Wynn (2000) suggest that when asked to describe who we are, we invariably include information about the different groups to which we belong—family, sports, religious, town, clubs, etc. However, not every group is a team and not every team is effective. In other words, everyone must agree on a goal and agree that the only way to achieve that goal is to work together in order to be an effective team.

Teams have an assortment of goals that vary from winning a game, to conducting a research project, to having the most productivity output. Regardless of their form, what they are called, or what their goals are, teams have to consider a multitude of factors. Among the important factors are cooperation and consensus, which are needed among all team members. Cooperation is having an association that leads to a mutual end result, benefiting all parties involved (Huber, 1980).

Whether it is a mission, goal, or task, a team must know why it exists and what it should be doing at the end of a meeting, by the end of the quarter, or a year from now. There is nothing more frustrating than being part of a group that meets with no sense of why they have come together. The best method to avoid this situation is to have an effective training program for people who are being placed on teams.

The Importance of Teams in the Future

Teams will become an important part of the organizational environment in the future in the slimmed down organizations of today. This is supported by research that shows, in particular, three performance advantages of teams: 1) when the presence of an expert is uncertain, groups seem to make better judgments than average individuals; 2) when problem solving can be handled by a division of labor and the sharing of information, groups are typically more successful than individuals; and 3) because groups tend to make riskier decisions than individuals, groups can be more creative and innovative in their task accomplishments (Shaw, 1976). One of the most salient reasons for the increasing use of teams is that teams get things done! More than solving problems, teams can be used to create value to the interaction with customers.

A prediction from Capezio (1998) summarizes why more teams will be used in the future. Capezio indicates that teams will be more prevalent because:

- The flattened organizations resulting from layoffs and downsizing will have fewer levels of authority and fewer resources available. Although this will result in less promotions, it will also result in greater opportunities to make decisions and a greater amount of employee self-management.
- Extraordinary pressure will be focused on maximizing productivity from everyone in the organization. As a result, employees will have a greater opportunity to contribute to not only their own success, but to the organization's success as well.
- The new technology gains place burdens on employees as information is more abundant and faster. As the distribution of information increases, more employees will be able to make decisions. As a result, employees will become more positive and productive.
- Employees will not be assigned to specific jobs or departments, but will become members of teams. As a result, the number of teams will increase dramatically.

Internet teams are becoming the preferred way of operating. The main value of teams is their ability to assemble and empower employees to use their talents to improve the efficiency and effectiveness of the organization to achieve the vision of making it a world-class operation. Because these functions are requirements for competing in the new business environment to drive costs out of organizations.

The Ultimate Glimpse into the Future . . . Virtual Teams??

What will the twenty-first century bring? With the acceptance and utilization of technology occurring at light speed, teams will become part of the technology revolution too. With less people, link-ups across the far reaches of the globe in milliseconds, and the coming of the global marketplace through Internet sites, teams will be utilized on a global basis. Virtual teams combining the best skilled people in the company regardless of their location around the world can join forces instantaneously through global networking.

According to Townsend, DeMarie, and Hendrickson (1996), relocations, temporary assignments, frequent travel, or use of external, local consultants could become things of the 1900s in only a few short years. Through new software, more powerful communication and connection systems, organizations will be able to create virtual teams. These virtual teams, located in different parts of the globe can have virtual meetings, or *cybermeetings*. With this virtual connectivity, team members can interact meaningfully over great distances with the same functionality of a face-to-face meeting.

Engleberg and Wynn (2000) indicate that these cybermeetings will include a growing list of technological team meeting tools. These tools can include the following:

- Software
- Instantaneously and simultaneously scheduling meetings on team members' calendars around the world
- Working white boards that can record and display information in multiple locations
- Internal information data ports in meeting rooms so that team participants can easily access databases
- Modules with complete electronic support systems (computer, fax, scanner, printer, etc.)

Thus, as the new generations of virtual Internet users become corporate managers, they will easily accept this approach to meetings. A camera on everyone's PC will bring Big Brother directly into everyone's office by visually linking counterparts and team members around the world.

Soon, traditional top management will rationalize acceptance of this new approach based on their cost-saving mentality—less time out of the office, less travel expenses, etc. The new, virtual team members will accept it as being nothing new and give new meaning to the old adage "we've always done it this way."

Chapter 2
Make Teams Part of Your Culture and Organizational Structure

Make a Team-Friendly Culture!

Developing a culture that places a premium on teams is no small task. Establishing and maintaining a team structure requires major organizational and cultural changes and commitment. Without a team mentality and pervasive acceptance from the CEO, the person running a manufacturing line and everyone in between, teams will not succeed. Without total acceptance, implementing a team orientation can turn into a management-directed nightmare. Teams thrive in a culture of trust and empowerment at all levels and among all employees. They not only must have the active support of top management, but top management also must be willing to walk the talk to make it happen. Otherwise, the poor implementation of a team orientation from this lack of real commitment from management will result in disaster. It will set back employee involvement, motivation, and productivity for years. The author of this book lived through such a situation; it was not a pretty experience.

It Takes a Real Commitment . . . or Else!

There are several reasons why teams fail. To start with, organizations might adopt teams for the wrong reason. Teams do not replace lost employees due to downsizing.

Interdivisional or interdepartmental squabbling might erupt. Without some control points built into the team structure, "turf wars" can break out. Instead of accomplishing tasks, teams become the pawns in political power struggles.

When teams are established for the wrong reasons and without good structure, there are problems. For example, a member of top management reads an article about how great teams are to produce new growth through new products. So, now everyone is on an innovation team. This may result in a quick fix mentality that is doomed from the beginning.

Sometimes, top management doesn't understand the needs of teams. They abdicate the responsibility of activities to teams without proper support. Teams get destroyed trying to resolve issues of authority, power, focus, and leadership.

Some members of top management only give lip service to teams. In practice they still revert to the top-down hierarchy of decision making. Worse yet, some managers continue to make all the decisions—with or without the team's agreement!

Another problem team members experience is a lack of adequate training. The sudden empowering of employees who always have been told what to do and when to do it without first preparing them for such empowerment is a recipe for disaster. Teams need training in all sorts of issues to be effective.

Team consensus in decision making does not compute for hierarchical leaders who are accustomed to the power and privileges that come with high rank and to making unilateral decisions. This lack of saliency for top management to relinquish the status and power that has taken them all of their career to build will not work.

Top management cannot just superimpose a team environment unilaterally and expect it to work. It takes application of the basic four tenets of the management process: organization, planning, control, and leadership. These tenets must be in place in the team structure if teams are to successfully replace a hierarchical organization structure.

How to Start? Get a Team Mentality!

Harrington (1995) indicated that before a team can even begin to work on the task at hand, three objectives should be identified as a way of life within the organization.

1. Team mission. Why the team exists
2. Team goals. What the team hopes to accomplish
3. Team guidelines. How the team will manage and measure itself

PRACTICAL TIP 1

Develop a team infrastructure to facilitate successful team operations.

Paramount to the effectiveness of a team-oriented organizational environment is providing an efficient and organized operating structure to facilitate the managing of all teams. A team management infrastructure within the organization must be established to control all of the teams effectively. One approach to an effective infrastructure is an inverted triangle with three distinct points of responsibility, but without any beginning or end. In essence, the triangle illustrates a closed, perpetual flow of team-related activities, which is a process designed to ensure team effectiveness across all venues in the organization.

A disciplined process to an operating team management infrastructure is Keen's Team Effectiveness Triangle©. Keen's triangle has a Lead Team supporting a Team Champion and Individual Teams in the organization as in the following diagram:

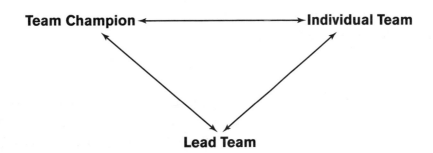

Keen's Team Effectiveness Triangle©

The Lead Team

The pivotal point of Keen's triangle is the Lead Team. The Lead Team is located at the bottom of the triangle because it provides the underpinning of support for the other two points of the triangle. This control point oversees management and provides overall leadership to the operation of the organization's entire team system. More importantly, it is *not* a council made up of top executives as a means to control what teams are doing.

The main responsibly of this group is to maintain an organizational-wide view of all of the team's activities to eliminate duplicity of activity. They have the sole authority in the organization to sanction the work and the establishment of any team. Most importantly, this group communicates to the rest of the organization the commitment, importance, and priority of the team system. This group is made up of a representation of all levels of both salaried management and hourly workers within the organization. The Lead Team must be convened by the CEO to demonstrate top management approval and support of the team system. All members of the Lead Team must be considered as having equal rank. This is required to avoid senior management manipulation, disruption, or control for their own self-interests.

The Lead Team acts as a steering committee to guide and nurture all team functions within the organization. It must portray a climate of confidence in the team management system and a sense of empowerment from the organization that supports the teams whether they succeed or fail. The Lead Team should meet as often as appropriate (from once a week for a firm with a significant number of teams to, at a minimum, once a month). This body should be charged by the CEO to accomplish the following goals:

1. Oversee the team process, not the specific results of each team
2. Provide organizational leadership, recognition, and focus for all teams
3. Oversee and allocate the resources of the entire organization in terms of personnel allocated to team activities, funding for team programs (e.g., research, external consultants, etc.), allocation of physical facilities (e.g., places for teams to conduct business), etc.

4. Approve the formation of each new team and specifically approve each team's goals, objectives, and timelines, and, more importantly, operating boundaries
5. Act as the control point for allocation of specific individuals to specific team activities
6. Act as the final arbitrator to resolve conflicts between teams and departments when priorities for members' time and resources are at variance
7. Provide a coordination point for monitoring every team's mission or charter and what each team is pursuing in order to eliminate any duplication of efforts
8. Provide a coordination point for knowledge sharing to improve the interaction and communication between teams that normally may not interface with each other
9. Act as the disseminator of project information throughout the organization as efficiently as possible, especially when such action is appropriate to quell rumors or to control the flow of communication throughout the organization
10. Provide the review point for teams to identify their progress, issues, and requests (e.g., for additional human or financial resources, etc.)
11. Provide a formal forum for teams to report the results and status of their decisions
12. Identify zones of operation (i.e., identifiable boundaries) for each team, as well as opposition to a team's area of activity concentration, and supply that information as feedback to all teams

The Team Champion

Another key point on the triangle is the Team Champion. This person is a representative of the division, department, manufacturing line, or other entity that directly benefits from the team's output. The key responsibility of the Team Champion is recognition of a need. That person must come to the team prepared to define the requirements and the exact results that are expected in a team mission or charter. The Team Champion must be able to articulate what the final state of the team's output will be in terms of the benefit to the entire organization. Most importantly, the Team Champion must ensure that the team mission or charter is in concert with the overall strategy of the organization. The Team Champion's additional roles are to help members understand any relevant large-scale organizational issues, be supportive of members' individual efforts, lend priority and credibility for the team's work throughout the organization, and act as the buffer and networker for the team with other stakeholders in the organization.

The Team Champion must present these roles as rational in a meeting with the Lead Team and receive agreement to proceed. The Team Champion is also responsible for ensuring that all of the organizational resources (financial, physical plant requirements, specific team training, additional human resources, etc.) required for the team to meet its goals is approved and allocated by the Lead Team.

By accepting the role of Team Champion, this individual also accepts additional responsibilities relative to ensuring that the team succeeds (Felts, 1995). The Team Champion must be available to the team as needed to clarify and correct the team's direction. The

Team Champion must also negotiate with the Individual Team a timetable for completion (probably not at the first team meeting). They must negotiate with the Lead Team and the Individual Team to identify what evaluation or measurement tools will be used to determine successful completion of the team's mission or charter. In addition, the Team Champion must be the two-way conduit between the Lead Team and the Individual Team. They must be willing to take requests to the Lead Team for any additional resources the team feels is required to complete the mission or charter and get approval for those resources. The champion assumes the roles of buffer, interpreter, and blocker for the team with the Lead Team. The Team Champion must be the lead communication link to report on the progress, status, and results of the team to the Lead Team and must provide evaluation and feedback to the team from the Lead Team. For instance, if there is a change in corporate strategy that affects the team, the team must be notified of the change as soon as possible to avoid being out of sync with the direction of the organization.

Once agreement to proceed has been received, it is the Team Champion's responsibility to articulate the approved benefit, deliverable, or objective to the team in the form of a mission or charter. No team can function effectively without a clear-cut charter. The Team Champion leads the team at its first meeting to lay out the expectations for team results. If appropriate, the Team Champion may become part of the team and act as the team leader. If the original Team Champion does not join the team, then a new team leader is elected by the team to fill the role of Team Champion. However, if the Team Champion does not join the team, sometime after the team has started working on the project, the team can request another meeting to revisit with the original Team Champion to review expectations or discuss any questions, issues, or suggested directions for the team's mission or charter.

This disciplined process avoids teams being created in a vacuum and avoids the creation of teams on an ad hoc basis that are self-serving to one department, division, or group and not the best use of the talent within the organization.

The Individual Team

The third point on the triangle is the Individual Team. Its function is to achieve the desired result as requested by the Team Champion. Because it deals directly with the Team Champion, the team does not have to deal with the bureaucratic or hierarchical influences coming from the Lead Team or within the organization so it can function autonomously to achieve its mission or charter.

PRACTICAL TIP 2
....

Match the mission or charter with the appropriate kind of team.

As indicated in chapter one, there are numerous ways and terminology to describe or label a team. Whatever teams are labeled, all of the descriptions seem to center on the end-point or final impact that the team will have on the organization. These end-points can be translated into three distinctly different kinds of teams: a Strategic Team, an Operation Team, and a Tactical Team. If the team's mission or charter will bring about a new direction in the way the organization does business in the future, then a Strategy Team is needed. If the team's mission or charter will bring about a change in the way the organization conducts its business, then an Operation Team is needed. If the team's mission or charter will bring about new improvements in the way the organization functions, then a Tactical Team is needed.

A *Strategic Team* is needed if the task concerns the future state of the organization. Strategic Teams determine strategic goals by monitoring changes and trends in the external environment, evaluating internal operations, and identifying critical priorities to get the organization to its prescribed future state. This high-level team is constituted with strategically oriented and experienced people who understand the complexities of designing such an encompassing task. For instance, such a task established by the Board of Directors as the Team Champion might be to design a long-term strategic merger and acquisition plan. Typical Strategic Team tasks include entering or exiting markets, investing in new technology, building manufacturing capacity, or forming strategic alliances. However, Strategic Teams do not focus on how to make decisions or complete specific activities.

An *Operation Team* is needed if the task is designed to contribute to the organization's growth or profits over the year term. Operation Teams will end up creating the execution of a Strategic Team's output. This team is usually constituted with cross-functional talents that enable the organization to examine the task from a multinational or multidivisional perspective. For example, if projected growth requires a new plant, an Operations Team would be formed to decide where, when, and how to build that plant.

However, if the task of a team involves an aspect of the work the organization does, then a *Tactical Team* is appropriate. Tactical Teams usually focus on functional jobs, such as planning and scheduling work activities. They usually focus on analyzing specific projects and how to take action on the projects. These teams are usually small groups of employees who have the technical or functional expertise to complete a specific task. For instance, if the task is to review a particular plant's operational procedure of a manufacturing line built to produce one specific product, then the composition of the team would be dramatically different from a Strategic or Operation Team.

But . . . Teams Are Not the Ubiquitous Solution

Two Harvard Business School professors, Katzenbach and Smith (1993), indicate that teams are not the solution to every current or future organizational need. Teams will not solve every problem, enhance every group's effort, nor help members of top management address every challenge. On the contrary, Katzenbach and Smith state that if misapplied, teams can be both wasteful of resources and disruptive to the company. The use of teams is analogous to playing golf or learning how to play the piano: without a commitment throughout the organization to practice, practice, practice, teams will not succeed within an organization.

Chapter 3
Teams Are Not the Quick Fix

Give the Teams Time to Develop: The Classical Approach to How Teams Evolve

Developing teams as a way of life in the organization takes time. Employees, assembled to accomplish a project, need time to gel together into an effective unit. Most books or articles on teams and team management refer to the classic approach (Tuckman, 1965) of the five stages in the team development model. The five stages are: forming, storming, norming, performing, and adjourning.

This model is sequential, developmental, and thematic. The *forming stage* of a team involves becoming committed to group goals and getting acquainted with the other team members. In this stage, members gain initial awareness that they are now a team. They also are briefed on why the team was formed and what is the team's mission or charter. This gives meaning to the team's existence. Not only do individuals need to understand how the team fits within the organization, but they also need to understand how they are related to the team's goals. Stage two is the *storming stage* where members become accustomed to being part of a team, and begin to assert themselves. This part of team development requires acknowledging and confronting conflict openly and listening with understanding to others. The third stage is the *norming stage* of team development where there is a clear shift from competition to collaboration among members. It involves including others in the decision-making process and recognizing and respecting individual differences and relationships. By this stage, collaboration becomes a team norm, and a feeling of genuine mutual support develops. Members should be able to give and receive feedback. In the fourth stage, known as the *performing stage* of team development, team members become loyal to the team and less dependent upon one leader. Members are encouraged to contribute ideas and solutions and to value the contributions and ideas of others. The last stage, the *adjourning stage* of team development, mostly occurs for teams that have a specified lifetime. It also might occur when a major task is completed or when major, new team members are added. An

17

evaluation of team accomplishments provides important feedback regarding job performance and working relationships.

This documentation of team history can be used to plan future ventures involving other teams. This also provides a sense of closure for the group and allows individuals to either say good-bye or commit to a future of further collaboration.

PRACTICAL TIP 3

Discover the new paradigm of how teams evolve.

Today, teams evolve quite differently than in the past, reflecting the casual atmosphere that is pervasive in business today. Out are old stuffed white shirts. In today's business environment, casual attire has moved from a dress-down Friday affair to an everyday way of life for many companies.

In order to reflect that casual approach to business a new paradigm is appropriate for how teams evolve among themselves. This new paradigm reflects the same casual work activity and a more people-friendly approach to the team formation process.

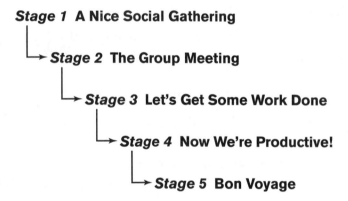

Stage 1 A Nice Social Gathering

Stage 2 The Group Meeting

Stage 3 Let's Get Some Work Done

Stage 4 Now We're Productive!

Stage 5 Bon Voyage

**Keen's New Paradigm
Team Formation Model©**

Stage 1: A Nice Social Gathering

Envision how you feel entering a party with a room full of people who you have never met or with whom you are only casually acquainted. This can feel pretty weird. That is how most people feel during the first meeting of a team. It's like saying to yourself at that party, "Why am I here?", "I don't know anybody," or "I really had something else I wanted to do anyhow." People tend to be polite in dealing with other team members and begin to look for leadership to answer the question "What am I going to bring to the team?" However, once members get acclimated to the team, they start getting excited and enthusiastic about being there—hopefully.

This stage is where team members get to know each other and feel each other out. Just like at the party, people ask each other things like "What's your name?", "What do you do?", or "Do you come here often?" To avoid this feeling, members must find out why they are there at the first meeting before beginning to define their personal team identities. It is imperative during this stage that the team focus on clarifying team goals and priorities to make it a productive session.

Stage 2: The Group Meeting

The next stage is when the awkward aspects of personality and intra-team relationships begin to work through the team. This stage is normally characterized by conflict and confusion, resulting in a lowering of team enthusiasm. Ideally this stage does not last long. However, in today's competitive world, this stage is important to the team's success and, more importantly, to its survival. If the team members cannot work themselves out, then friction, conflict, and jealousy—all ingredients for team failure—will prevail.

On the plus side, if the team leadership and members are proactive, getting through this stage can be productive in allowing the team members to begin asserting themselves, resulting in the development of a higher comfort level.

Stage 3: Let's Get Some Work Done

In today's fast-paced work environment, nobody really has time to waste. In the age of downsizing, most employees are doing more than one person did in the 1990s. Therefore, usually, team members are anxious to get to stage three to get some work done. Translated into today's language, it's to justify the value added of the team and its contribution to the organization.

Also, it's important that this justification occurs. The problems of the last stage of conflict and even confusion should be overcome. Rather, the prevailing team attitude has to be a can do attitude, which is exemplified by confidence and security. Even some minor accomplishment, albeit small in comparison to the team's overall mission or charter, can make a team gel. Team members should by now be willing to trust each other. They should be looking to each others' contribution to be able to get something accomplished.

Stage 4: Now We're Productive!

This stage is unlike any other stage. It's the dipstick of true team performance. If there is a sense of excitement, commitment, enthusiasm, productivity, autonomy, initiative, and cohesion, then the team has achieved success in the process. The members have a loyalty to the team and a real sense of the group being a team—it becomes their team. Team pride and esprit de corps are highest at this stage. Productivity breeds a sense of self-worth and self-accomplishment for the team and for each member.

Stage 5: Bon Voyage

If you have ever been on an extended cruise or even been to an extended sleep-away camp, you know the feelings generated in stage five. There is excitement and joy of experiencing something positive. However, when the trip is over, you experience angst and sadness. Successful teams have this sense. Their specific deliverable has been achieved. Of note is that some team members might not want the experience to end and can have feelings of separation anxiety associated with this stage. However, the key in this stage is to rejoice in the team's success. The organization and the part of the organization that will benefit most from the team delivering its mission or charter must celebrate the team's success publicly within the organization. Team recognition and rewards are keys to maintaining a healthy team environment.

Establish a Sense of Purpose for Each Team

As stated earlier, to be successful, the team must understand all of the background as to why it was formed. An honest statement of why the team was formed translated into a team mission or charter statement must be developed for the team to understand the constraints and boundaries of its task. In addition, they need to be briefed on the scope of the project and its relationship to other team activities. The team must then take that information and develop a charter or statement of purpose from the very beginning of the project. By doing this, all team members can start to take ownership of the project by being part of defining the team's mission or charter from its inception.

Part of the team's formation process includes developing the specific objectives and timetable for the team. The members need to be trained on what is an objective and how to establish and prioritize the most important objectives. The team must understand the performance specifications and expectations in relation to the established timetable or specifically on what timeframe the team will be judged in order to be a success.

It is imperative that the team discusses and agrees on the boundaries and limitations within which it must exist. This provides focus and direction for the team in terms of what it should be doing and, importantly, what is outside of its purpose. This requirement is needed to avoid teams drifting aimlessly in search of what it should do. Training helps members ask questions and develop boundaries to avoid wasting time.

The team must be provided with all available information on its task. Either it should be given this data when it receives the mission or charter, or members of the team should be assigned to research available databases. This will avoid the team wasting valuable resources going over old ground or reinventing what already exists.

Each team should have a clear idea of who the customer is for the project. Whether the customer is internal (e.g., a plant line supervisor) or external (e.g., new client), the team should clearly understand who is to benefit by its project, task, or activity.

The Key Factors of Successful Teams

Based on extensive research into teams, the author of this book feels that one researcher has done a very credible effort to realistically and efficiently summarize the requirements of successful team formation. According to Bishop (1999), the following are 17 factors that go into creating and maintaining successful teams.

Project Sponsorship and Upper Management Support.   There needs to be a vehicle for employees to request that a team be developed within the organization. A place needs to be established to hold the budget and allocate resources. A cross-functional, organizational-wide steering committee is key and must be in place to monitor the progress of all teams in the organization.

Project Goals, Scope, and Objectives.   The project's merit to the organization and its link to corporate strategy and objectives must be clear. Each team must be aware of the expectations for its accomplishments.

Leadership.   There must be leader or captain established for each team who has a positive attitude and commitment to the project. The leader must have excellent organization, good coordination, and effective leadership skills.

Membership and Resources.   Adequate team staffing, resources (e.g., finances), and considerations of employee time are critical to the success of any team. The prevailing key organizational mentality should be that team membership is a privilege for employees, not a penalty.

Communication.   All forms of communication (up, down, and across) the entire geographical and hierarchical structure of the organization are key to team success. This magnitude of communication is especially important to break down functional and physical boundaries when teams are first formed. Communications are key to managing the expectations and monitoring the progress of each team.

Team Authority and Autonomy.   Successful teams have very high levels of internal and external decision-making authority. They must also have both authority and accountability to accomplish their task, mission, or charter successfully. Teams need to feel that they have the final word in the recommendations that go forward to management. They must feel that they can have an opportunity to not only be part of the final decisions, but also to negotiate the final decisions.

Performance or Reward Systems. Members' performance must be evaluated and rewarded within the context of the organization's team infrastructure. The members' team performance must be equally important to the performance of their normal, daily jobs. Amount of time spent on team functions must be the driver to create the appropriate level of weight team performance has on the employee's overall performance evaluation. Some sort of team and team member recognition must be built into the organization's team philosophy.

Team Dynamics. Team members need to operate effectively as a team with mutual respect, open communication, and mutual accountability. They must deal comfortably with team conflict, challenges, and disagreements; be loyal to the team; be comfortable with consensual decision making; and feel that the right people were chosen for the appropriate teams.

Organizational Structure. Teams' structural requirements are different from hierarchical organization's structural requirements. Some sort of matrix must be built into any change to a team organization.

Organizational Type. Teams offer greater flexibility than larger organizational groups or designs. Smaller groupings are more appropriate for teams. Team members must become comfortable and be able to identify with both their home department and the team.

Project Ownership. Typically, the senior manager at the top of the hierarchy in which the team belongs becomes, by rank, the team "owner". However, teams are usually comprised of many different functional areas. The project owner must recognize and cope with the reality that team members have many competing responsibilities and will respond to the squeaky wheel for their attentions and effort.

"Turf" Issues. Team recommendations and output, especially from cross-functional teams, may be threatening to the domain of other areas of the organization. The greater the understanding of the individual team's function within the organization, the greater the impact it may have to cross "territorial" lines of authority and activities. An effective steering committee will ease these turf issues. This committee's role is to communicate to teams the overall direction of the organization and what role the specific team plays in the organization's plans and goals.

Chain of Command. Key is the need for team members to take responsibility to communicate back to their respective functional areas the pros and cons of all activities occurring in their teams. This cross-pollination of team activities up, down, and across the organization can yield significant productivity rewards.

Information Flow. Lack of adequate communication vehicles (e.g., team Web site) encourages mistrust, which is a breeding ground for the team being sabotaged both within and without. The steering committee must set an expectation that communication throughout the organization is a requirement and, equally important, the stacking of information by teams into their own silos within the organization is not tolerated. This is especially needed to quell rumors and misinformation when teams are working on key organizational issues and initiatives.

Resource Ownership. Team members usually will not be fully allocated to team activities and retain some responsibilities within their own functional areas. This may put the team in a position of continuously "selling" to team members a commitment to the team activities versus pressure to complete their "day jobs". Without some sort of continuous "selling," the members might yield to the pressures from their home departments and migrate back to addressing departmental activities to achieve their short-term milestones. If resource ownership and team reward or incentive structures are not adequately in place, then team members might feel that a greater sense of personal short- and long-term career gain is achieved by completing their assigned departmental tasks than working on team activities. This is another task for the steering committee, who must arbitrate between team and departmental priorities for team members' time and resources.

Individual Team Member Status. Hierarchical organization structures historically utilize the concept of rank. Organizational reward systems are built in to support the whole concept of rank. However, ranking within a team can result in the team becoming ineffective and can impede several benefits of teaming: collective thought, knowledge sharing, and group decision making. Equality among all team members is a basic and unalterterable tenant for the utilization of teams. Team building exercises, extensive team training, and team-based reward systems are needed to make a successful shift from the hierarchical organization structure to the team structure.

Assessment Reward Focus. Traditional employee performance appraisal and reward systems (e.g., bonuses and promotions in rank) are primarily geared toward individual achievement in a functionally oriented environment. Apparently, Bishop's (1999) research indicated that employees would like a mix of individual and team rewards. Employee surveys (Bishop, 1999) indicated that a system based on employees' departmental performance and the total team's performance proved to be most effective in promoting contributions to teams. More importantly, both formal and informal reward and recognition of the success of teams as a whole are key factors as effective team member incentives.

Be Prepared to Recognize Resistance to Teams

In addition to touting the success of teams, recognition must also be paid to resistance to teams. In the organization where teams are new, the inherent resistance to change is part of its change management process. However, there might be reluctance to teams in general that is pervasive in the organization.

Katzenbach and Smith (1993) indicated that although the argument for teams is compelling, many people are reluctant to rely on teams. They feel that there are three primary sources for reluctance to use teams.

1. *Lack of conviction.* Some do not inherently believe that teams really do perform better than individuals. Some believe that teams cause more trouble than value, because of wasted time in unproductive meetings.

2. *Personal discomfort and risk.* Many people fear, or simply do not like, working with a group of other people. There are some people, for example, scientists, who are loners and will work best when left alone. Most people do feel some anxiety about working in teams. This discomfort with teams might stem from the feeling that the team approach is a distraction or takes too much time away from employees' "day jobs". It might stem from too much uncertainty over the lack of control for the outcome. Some people just feel that teams are too risky, because they do not enable team members to achieve their personal career goals or timetable.

3. *Weak organizational performance ethics.* Some companies lack compelling purposes as to why teams are important to the long-term health and well-being of the organization. When that attitude is pervasive, there is more concern about internal politics or external public relations than a commitment to the goals of the organization. In the worst-case scenario, such an environment undermines the mutual trust and openness upon which teams depend. There is also an expectation that any decision of consequence must be made at the top or, at a minimum, be approved by several ascending layers within the organization.

These politics promote employee insecurity, which further erodes the conviction in and acceptance of teams among the employees. Hence, bad team experiences become the organization's self-fulfilling prophecy that teams will not work. There are deviations that will result in successful teaming, but they become real exceptions rather than the norm within these organizations. It is this link between teams and poor or unorthodox performance within these types of organizations that must be recognized and dealt with because it can breed resistance to teams.

Chapter 4
Let's Start with Teamwork

Teamwork Makes Teams Effective

What makes a team effective or ineffective? There are many characteristics that distinguish between effective teams and ineffective teams, and they all rely on teamwork!

Capezio (1998) indicates that winning teams have two common factors that rely on teamwork. First is the *task factor,* which is the ability of a team to accomplish what it is designed to do by having mutual goals. The second factor is *relationships,* which is where the team focuses on the one-to-one and intergroup collaboration dynamics that can help the productivity of the team.

Effective teams have a certain unity of feeling. Those team members enjoy being around the people of their team, look forward to the meetings, enjoy learning new things together, appear to have fun and laugh more than other teams, find themselves putting the team's assignments ahead of other work, and feel a real sense of progress and satisfaction.

Essentials of Teamwork

Now that team organizational structures, kinds of teams, and different team member types have been discussed, the next issue is bringing these factors together through teamwork. Let's start with the essentials of teamwork. These essentials include:

- An acceptance of the common goals of the team
- A hierarchy of leadership within the team that is either appointed or elected
- All members are able to get along, interact well, and involve each other in team business
- Open communication between all members and zero tolerance for hidden agendas
- The team senses and acts with a feeling of empowerment
- Everyone pays attention to both the process and the content of the team's activities
- Mutual trust among all members

- Respect for individual differences
- Constructive conflict resolution

PRACTICAL TIP 4

Know the seven characteristics of high-performing teams.

In the typical fashion of today's fast-paced world, another way to approach building team-work is based on *The One Minute Manager* series of books. Specific to dealing with team-work is the book titled *The One Minute Manager Builds High-Performing Teams* (Blanchard, 2000). It offers the PERFORM model to identify desired behaviors that consti-tute teamwork. The model details seven characteristics of high-performing teams using the PERFORM acronym as follows:

P   Purpose. Teams have a sense of purpose about what is the mission or charter of the team and why it is important to the organization. They have developed mutually agreed upon responsibilities, goals, and strategies to achieve those goals.

E   Empowerment. Teams have the confidence to overcome obstacles and realize their plans. They have mutual respect and shared responsibilities. Note: Additional elements of empowerment will be covered in the next section.

R   Relationship and communication. There is an atmosphere of trust and commitment among team members based on open communications, the ability to state opinions with-out fear, effective conflict management, and high group cohesion.

F   Flexibility. Members share team functional responsibilities as needed. The strengths of each member are leveraged. The team adapts to change because its members are fluid and open minded.

O   Optimal productivity. These teams produce significant results because they have a com-mitment to high standards within the team. The team has developed effective decision-making and problem-solving skills.

R   Recognition and appreciation. In addition to team successes, individual success is also celebrated. Members feel respected and well regarded by other team members.

M   Morale. Members maintain a high level of morale and enthusiasm. There is a sense of excitement and esprit de corps is high.

Essentials of Empowerment

As Blanchard (2000) and others indicate, teamwork is driven by team members feeling em-powered to act and make decisions. By definition, empowerment means giving authority and enabling members to act on their own. This is the opposite of the bureaucratic concept of authority, which means having the power to force people to act.

Authority in an empowered organization means the individual or team has the power to get things done. Inherent in successfully using empowerment in a team environment is that the team or team member has the ability to recognize problems and take action. Teams must not only feel comfortable with authority and power, but also be willing to take responsibility for their actions and the results of their actions. Therefore, team members must understand that under the old hierarchical way, authority meant power. Under the team concept, power means the ability to take action to get something accomplished.

PRACTICAL TIP 5

Success equals empowerment.

After studying one hundred teams, Kirkman and Rosen (2000) concluded that a sense of empowerment is closely associated with teamwork and team success. They articulated four main attributes that winning and empowered teams share.

1. A Sense of Potency.   A winning team shares a sense of the team's capabilities. Members exhibit a confident, can-do attitude. As a result, they are likely to take on additional responsibilities and desire higher levels of decision-making freedom. Internally, they display much more confidence and team assuredness in their meetings and, importantly, they speak in *we* terms instead of *I* terms.

2. A Sense of Meaningfulness.   Winning teams share a sense of how the teamwork affects them. Members are more likely to care about their individual spot on the team and their team responsibilities. They have a strong collective commitment to the team's mission or charter. They see the work of their team as valuable and worthwhile and they view even the most mundane aspects of their team jobs as integral to the overall success of the team.

3. A Sense of Autonomy.   Winning teams share a feeling of freedom, discretion, and control. Autonomous teams feel like they can establish their own work processes, have the freedom to allocate resources, seize opportunities, and make rapid decisions without continuously seeking higher-level approval.

4. A Sense of Impact.   Winning teams can visualize the effect of their labors on other stakeholders. This sense of team satisfaction further drives members' enthusiasm. Feedback from customers, stakeholders, and Team Champions are important for these teams to maintain their momentum.

So, How Does a Team Champion Impact Teamwork?

Teamwork begins with the Team Champion asserting him- or herself as the leader of the team. As the leader, the Team Champion should be intensely involved with the work of the team. Most importantly, as the leader, the Team Champion sets the tone and should be the role model for the rest of the team. As the overall team leader, this person is responsible for keeping the team on course toward reaching its mission or charter.

The title of *Team Champion* is not in itself an important term. What is important is that the individual is trained in accepting the leadership role. Importantly, the Team Champion must understand what is leadership. *Leadership* can be defined as the ability to persuade others to achieve defined objectives enthusiastically. Leadership is simply getting others to want to do what must be done. Leadership is different than management. Leadership complements management, it does not replace it. The difference is in the distinction of getting others to do and getting others to *want* to do a project, task, or effort.

In order to lead a team, the Team Champion needs to hone or develop as well as practice demonstrating several qualities that go into making a leader.

- Challenging the process by taking risks. Being an innovator by experimenting with new ways of doing things is very desirable. In addition, leaders should challenge others to generate good ideas and support those who challenge the system to get things done despite the risk of failure.
- Inspiring a shared vision to make something happen. This means having a clear vision from the project's outset of what the end result will be. Leaders should not look to anyone else to breathe life into the team's vision and inspire others to share and work at turning that vision into reality.
- Empowering others to be part of the team. Leaders should make others comfortable with feeling a sense of ownership by collaborating on teams. They are the "cheerleader" to involve, enlist support, and elicit assistance to make the project happen. In addition, they gain this support by having others feel strong, capable, and committed to the project or empowered to act on their ownership of the project. They make team members deal in the *we* state instead of the *I* state.
- Modeling the way. The leader should practice what he or she preaches. In other words, they lead by example and be a role model for the other team members.
- Encouraging others. This encouragement is needed especially to carry on even in the face of adversity. Most importantly, leaders should recognize the individuals' contributions to the team and be sure to celebrate their accomplishments—however small or large they may be. They show members how they can win, not how they can lose.

How Does a Team Champion Impact the Team?

Leading the team means following five simple steps that should ensure teamwork. First, the Team Champion must passionately lead the team toward its mission or charter as the clear end-point for the team by answering the question: What needs to be done to achieve success? This passion is translated into clear goals that can be used to motivate team members to achieve that vision. The Team Champion must work with the team to identify milestones (not penalties) that will show how, when, and where progress toward these goals can be measured. When a milestone is achieved, acknowledge it, celebrate it, and publicize it! Take time out to let people know how to feel good about achieving a milestone.

Second, use teamwork as the means of delegating workload to groups of people. This can mean a shift in the Team Champion's mentality. This shift in mental states may be required as the team moves from the traditional, hierarchical, bureaucratic structure to more of a hub structure with the Team Champion at the center of the team. Once this mental adjustment has been made, a major hurdle for the group's development of teamwork will occur.

Third, as indicated earlier in this book, empowerment is very important in developing teamwork. To *empower* usually means to give power or authority, to authorize, to enable or permit. Thus, in order to empower members, the Team Champion should begin to lead—not do all of this teamwork themselves. It is key to involve the team in goal setting, not to dictate the team's goals. When the champion dictates, it defeats the purpose of empowerment and lowers teamwork among the members.

Fourth, aim for consensus. This means the Team Champion helps team members move toward general agreement. It is key to foster consensus throughout the teaming process, not only at one point in the process. The team members must be able to have some ownership of tasks that need to be done and consensus helps achieve that end.

The last step is to direct the process, not the work. This requires experience in working with teams and knowledge about exactly what teamwork is all about. Effective Team Champions use a number of techniques to help the team get the work done, but do not do the work themselves.

If these facilitation skills are lacking or if teamwork is not forthcoming, immediately send the Team Champion to team leadership training. Do not let the Team Champion learn under the fire of battle or the team is doomed to failure.

Guidelines for Effective Teamwork

There are a number of key activities that result in effective teamwork. First, the team must begin and continue to act as a whole, not separate parts. All team members must be open and honest with each other. They must all be open-minded and willing to try new things. They must stretch themselves by thinking outside of their own boxes. They must stay focused on the team's goals and not deviate from their course of action. They should enjoy each other's company and not belittle others on the team. Lastly, the team should enjoy what it is doing and have fun doing it.

Effective Team Interpersonal Relationships

There are a number of appropriate attitudes that are important among team members in order to have successful teamwork. Team attitudes are required to strengthen and maintain group activities. These teamwork attitudes include:

- Encouraging others. Being friendly, warm, responsive to others, praising others and their ideas, agreeing with and accepting the contribution of others.
- Gatekeeping effectively. Making it possible for every member to make a contribution to the team or suggesting limited talking time for everyone so that all have a chance to be heard.

- Standard setting. Suggesting standards for the team to use in choosing its content or procedures or in evaluating its decisions and reminding the group to avoid decisions that conflict with team standards.
- Following members' lead. Going along with the decision of the team, thoughtfully accepting ideas of others, and serving as an audience during team discussion.
- Expressing the sense of the team. Summarizing what the feeling of the team is sensed to be and describing reactions of the team to ideas or solutions.

Conversely, there are also a number of danger signals or inappropriate team attitudes. Inappropriate team attitudes cause division and unrest on the team. These inappropriate team attitudes are:

- Displays of aggression. Comments or actions that deflate other members' status or position or attack the team or its values.
- Blocking. Disagreeing and opposing beyond reason or being closed minded or stubborn.
- Domination. Members asserting authority or superiority in an attempt to control others or the team.
- Checking out. Having members mentally leave the team for extended periods of time, while physically being with the team.
- Child-like actions. Members seeking attention in ways that are not relevant to the team.
- Avoidance behaviors. Members supporting special interests or getting the team to stray from the task.

The Idea of Team Building

Team building helps to create successful teamwork. The term *team building* refers to a procedure by which planned action steps are created with the purpose of designing and gathering information on the functioning of the team and implementing changes, when needed, based on the team's consensus. The goal here is to improve the team's effectiveness (Szilagyi & Wallace, 1990). Steps common to this are as follows:

- A member or members notice an existing or developing problem.
- The group gathers information on the problem, works together to analyze the data, and makes plans for improvement.
- The group works together to implement the plans, monitor progress, evaluate results, and take further action if necessary (Schermerhorn, Hunt, & Osborn, 1994).

Many teams use the team building concept to help clarify core values, which helps to guide and direct the members, or to diagnose the information, task accomplishment, team relationships, and the organization of the team (Szilagyi & Wallace, 1990).

A Four-Step Method for Team Building Strategy

Tolle (1988) offered the following approach to building teamwork:

1. All members must understand and agree on the mission or purpose of the team effort from the start.
2. Each unit should have goal statements that are visible, concise, and relevant.
3. Objectives should be developed that are attached to the mission and the goals that they support.
4. Responsibility charting, which involves the activities of responsibility, approval, support, and information, should be part of the team-building process.

In team building, members work together to achieve desired goals and objectives. In successful teams, members are challenged to work to their greatest potential in order to create teamwork. A major concern at this stage is sustaining momentum and enthusiasm. Complex goals and objectives require the creation of incremental steps and subgoals. The establishment of milestones or benchmarks for success at such points and the celebration when these points are reached contribute both to motivation and team revitalization.

PRACTICAL TIP 6

Know the seven steps to achieve successful teamwork.

Based on its experience with many organizations, the Quality Alert Institute has developed some common steps required to set up and run effective teams. The seven steps to maintain successful teamwork are as follows:

1. Set up a head team to guide and nurture the team structure and operation. The head team's responsibility is to maintain a top-level view of all of the team's activities to eliminate duplicity of activity. As a result, they have the responsibility and authority to sanction the work and the establishment of a team. More important, the head team's role is to provide reassurance to the organization that this approach can (or will) work.

   Head team members must lead by example and be staunch advocates for the team process. They must be able to communicate their enthusiasm for the team system throughout everything they do, everyday. The most important contribution of this team is empowerment. The teams must feel that the empowerment is real and that top management will support their decisions. This trust level, empowerment, and delegation of power is sometimes difficult for top management to give up. However, it is the key that unlocks the successful use of teams.

2. The organization must establish a process orientation. Widely available, easy-to-read charts tracking work, rework, schedules, and so on, must abound around the

organization. Only this process approach provides the internal mechanism for the team to become and stay self-managed.

3. Although by its charter the organization has a customer orientation, everyone, top to bottom, must understand the customer's requirements in detail. Everyone must understand that its customers are both inside (internal) and outside (external) the company. This means the orientation must include finding out what customers really want, need, value, and, most importantly, expect from the team. One way to accomplish this is to conduct internal and external customer surveys and flowchart the processes, opportunities, and problems that will allow the team to achieve its desired results.

4. A sense of teamwork within the organization must become the standard operating procedure, not the exception.

5. An entirely new system of reward and performance evaluations must be instituted and adhered to within the organization. This new system is critical for allowing team members to take responsibility for process management and improvement and changing the way they have historically viewed their jobs.

6. Everyone must recognize that the team approach to management is not the way employees have been doing their jobs historically. Employees must have positive guidance and assistance from their supervisors to make this transition from the old way to the new way. People will need help to learn that teamwork means giving support, feedback, and encouragement to make others comfortable and secure. The team structure outlined in chapter three must be put in place to effect this change or the whole change process will take much longer than necessary and create enormous frustrations.

7. All team members must be trained to prepare themselves for this new way of work life. Because there are no "bosses" on teams, everyone on the team must learn and be willing to accept unprecedented team-oriented authority, responsibility, and decision making. Everyone must be trained in process-improvement techniques, problem solving, interactive skills, and process methodologies such as flowcharting.

What to Look for to See if Teamwork Is Really There

A sense of belonging is key to building successful teams. Team members have to communicate and motivate each other to cope with the changing business environment. Teamwork, which includes communication, motivation, trust, goal identification, and other human interaction skills, determines the success of leaders and their organizations in this new work unit.

Communication is important for all types of organizations. In order to establish successful team communication, there must be a genuine trust and shared interest between the parties. To be successful and keep an ongoing relationship, people should not judge a person or discourage her or him from taking the risk of communicating again. If there is an exchange of ideas among group members, those members have taken a risk to express their opinions. It is imperative to keep the lines of communication open in order to achieve a harmonious atmosphere among team members. This type of interaction is not easy because it involves putting one's ideas out in the open. It takes patience, work, and time, but it can be done.

Another factor needed to ensure successful teamwork is motivation. Everyone wants a paycheck or an end-of-the-year-bonus, but the real motivation for success is emotional satisfaction. People who are motivated only by a paycheck will only work as hard as they have to in order to get paid. A person must want to work hard for the sake of the team. Successful group motivation comes from working toward a mutually important goal. Successful teamwork recognizes, includes, encourages, and praises people, and lets them make decisions.

John Dewey, considered by some to be among one of the United States' most profound philosophers, said that the deepest urge in human nature is the desire to be important (Carnegie, 1993). People will only perform if they feel as though they are an important part of the team. To feel important, members have to be involved in aspects of the group process.

Two other important characteristics needed to be successful in a team are the abilities to express genuine interest in others and see things from the other person's point of view. Everyone likes to talk about themselves. People respond to those people who are interested in them. We are all flattered when someone is paying attention to us; it makes people feel good when you show interest in them. This builds a trusting relationship that will assist you in seeing things from other people's points of view. A team is made up of people who want to share their ideas and feelings on a given subject. If these people feel comfortable with the members of their team, there is more of a chance for the group to be successful through active communication.

There are many elements that are needed to make teamwork successful on a team, such as cooperation and consensus. Without these factors, an unbalanced team may not be able to accomplish the goals that were assigned, leading to the dissolution of the teams and cancellation of projects. Teams must work hard on team building when they are faced with tasks and goals to accomplish (Szilagyi & Wallace, 1990).

Another dimension of achieving success requires diversity on the team to give it a competitive advantage. Each member should bring unique talent, style, and ideas to the group. Diverse gender or ethnic backgrounds, for example, can bring new perspectives to group decisions.

Successful teams are not sidetracked with irrelevant material. They focus on the task that needs to be accomplished and use time wisely, not for socializing purposes. This does not mean that the team cannot socialize outside of the meetings, but that team time should be used only to accomplish the team purposes. During meetings, the team should keep track of how much progress has been made. They also should pace themselves on how much time is spent on each topic. Key information also should be reviewed at the beginning and end of each meeting (Aubrey, 1988).

Teamwork establishes interdependence among members that should lead to a trusting relationship in which members have respect for each other as well as the assignment or task with which they are faced (Cohen & Cohen, 1984). The power, recognition, and status that are achieved through group membership, in general, motivate successful teams. These successful groups come to recognize that there is a vast amount of knowledge contained in other individuals. Gaining this knowledge, which can only be accessed through interaction with the other members, has to involve cooperation and consensus among the parties (Aubrey, 1988).

Chapter 5
Teams Start with People

Teams Are People, Too!

Having a team organizational structure is important, but the most important issue when dealing with teams is how to make sure that each team is staffed with the most appropriate people for each type of team. Having the right people working on the right teams does not occur by accident. One basic principle of successful organizations is to take effective advantage of the various abilities, backgrounds, and interests of its human assets. Cooperation is not just something that would be nice for a company; it is essential for its success. Only if employees work together to solve problems and complete tasks can organizations really be productive.

Therefore, people make or break an organization; they are its most important resource. People are more important than a company's products or technology. People, after all, decide the products and services to offer, the tools to be used to make the products, and the strategies to market products. Understanding how people work together is extremely important and has a great practical payoff—a successful organization.

The Easiest Way to Select Team Members

The easiest way, and the worst way, for an organization to allocate employees to teams is to assign employees by availability or seniority. The employees who are not on other teams could be used as the pool to draw from when developing a new team. The plus to using this approach is that all employees can have a chance to be on a team. The problem is that all employees do not make good team members and could be a drain on the rest of the team because they cannot contribute or "pull their weight" on the team. Therefore, this is neither an effective nor a viable way to select team members.

Or Select Only Good "Team Players"

The next easiest way to select members for teams is to choose those employees who have a proven track record of being very comfortable on a team. These are probably employees who have already shown a propensity to work well in teams. The plus for this approach is that the person has already shown the ability to provide value added to a team. The argument against this approach is that past performance might not be a good indicator of future performance unless the person fills the same role, possibly with only the same people, on the same type of team as before. If the employee does not perform well on additional team assignments, they might develop a confidence problem, which can negatively impact their overall performance.

Hold an Auction

Another way to assemble teams is for managers to gather and negotiate the makeup of a team. For example, managers can come to a meeting with a list of people they want to put on teams. However, interesting motivations can exist with this auction approach. Managers can use teams as punishment for not being loyal to the manager or for not completing a project or, in a worst case rationale, for embarrassing the manager in some way. Managers simply might want the employee out of the way or out of the department because of internal personality conflicts. Managers might be trying to get rid of the employee, even though they are aware of the team's task and know that it would be a stretch for the employee and is a recipe for failure. The manager might also be using the employee as a political pawn to accomplish something totally unrelated to the team's activity from other managers in the team selection meeting.

The Simple Solution!

If these three no brainer approaches do not work, then what? Some managers decide to run the team. If that seems like a good idea, then ask this question: Is that what the manager gets paid to do? The answer is no! If the manager diverts time and energy toward managing each team, then they will not have the time and energy to do their other tasks effectively and efficiently. Running teams takes time and will only add more stress to the daily work life. A manager's real job is to nurture and provide the direction for the department, not micromanage each team.

The Key That Unlocks the Secret of Selecting the Right Team Players

Building an effective team requires a reasonable supply of candidates and an adequate number of diverse talents to play defined team roles. It becomes an issue of casting the right players in the right roles to make the team successful. As in the film industry, it is not enough to assemble good actors and actresses. What is essential is that they are ideal for their parts. However, casting for an effective team is very difficult. Especially when there are severe time constraints, casting for team players using one of the previously mentioned approaches can be very attractive. It can also prove to be an economic disaster, just like in making a film. Each player must bring a different team orientation as well as a unique skills set. Orchestrated together, employees will work together in harmony and generate highly effective output. If this can be accomplished with a limited number of employees, so much the better.

A Better Way to Choose Team Members

An imbalance of team roles and personalities can shatter teamwork and be counterproductive to developing an effective and efficient team. This is especially true when teams are thrown together using one of the techniques mentioned earlier. If by some slim chance the employees put together on a team by one of these techniques are successful, it's usually because of other reasons. Without the right balance of roles and personalities, the team will fail.

Several theorists have posited that another way to select team members is to identify and fill specific team-player roles or personality styles that are required to make the team balanced. Davis (Davis et al., 1992) suggested the largest number of team roles as fifteen, while Parker suggested the least number of team roles as four (Parker, 1990). The identification of team roles has been based on different personality characteristics (Parker, 1990). Others theorists have identified team roles based on their observations of typical behaviors in various types of teams in many different organizations.

As an early proponent of the team role concept, the work of Belbin (1981, 1993) is particularly interesting because it appears it is the basis on which other team role frameworks have been built. Belbin has been considered the Father of Teams because of his work in this area of team roles. Belbin's development of the team role concept arose from observing, over a period of many years, teams of managers on training courses playing management games where team performance was measured in terms of winning or losing.

Based on his observations, Belbin identified nine team roles that he felt existed on each successful team. Belbin then constructed a survey to identify people with those various team roles that he felt were paramount to designing successful teams. He claimed to be able to predict the performance of a team through knowledge of each team member's team role.

Dr. Belbin has also developed a technique called *Interplace,* which identifies a person's propensity for one of these roles as being their primary team role. His technique also identifies a person's alternative or back-up team roles. This technique has been adapted to a short list of questions that can be answered in only a few minutes. Once the answers to the questions are processed using his computer model, a person's team role propensities will emerge.

The importance of this technique is that it provides a profile for all of the employees under consideration as potential team members. Armed with this information, it would become possible to cast teams with the correct configuration of players to make a team more productive because they will bring different, complementary personalities as well as skill sets to the team. This is an attempt to avoid the problem of having all one type of team member on one team.

Belbin's Hypothesis

Belbin first suggested in 1981 that a team of six people would be the most suitable size to enable a management team to tackle a complex problem. Because Belbin identified nine key roles, this proposal inherently implied that some team members need to operate in more than one role. The degree of difficulty for team members to operate in more than one role was addressed by Belbin (1981) when he indicated observing that most competent managers seem to be able to function in a team with some underlying construct (and possibly combinations). Belbin (1981) provided some insight into this issue when he indicated that the shaper and team worker were an unlikely combination, but implied that chairperson and team worker, plant and monitor evaluator, and team worker and company worker were combinations that probably would be found together.

His points were few and tentative, but he hypothesized that some basic principles exist that unify the team role model and that such principles could be identified. He felt that if these tendencies could be isolated, it would enable companies to make better predictions as to which roles their team members may require to form successful teams.

Based on this research conducted over a period of several years, Belbin posited that a team composed of very talented people does not perform as well as one which contains individuals who possess a good mix of the team member roles identified earlier. Belbin (1981) explained that about 30 percent of the individuals tested did not clearly fall into any of the categories and their contribution to team achievement and effectiveness was very limited. The other 70 percent could be classified into a team role. Each had a particular preference but most also had a secondary team role that they could play if the situation demanded. For example, if a member of the team is not performing a particular team role, then someone else might play that role in addition to the one for which he or she is best suited.

When all team roles are strongly represented across the profiles (making the team "balanced"), the team is predicted to be high performing. Where some team roles are absent, he maintained that the team will have a lower success rate.

Belbin's Team Types

Belbin's management team model described the ideal team as a group of individuals who could fulfill eight and later nine team roles that he had identified (Belbin, 1993).

The names and descriptions that follow the team roles may be a bit confusing, but it is important to remember that they are intended only as explanations of the personal characteristics displayed by someone in that role.

Coordinator. This person is mature, confident, balanced, and people oriented. They command considerable respect from the team, help clarify team goals, promote decision making, and are calm, confident, and self-controlled.

Plant. This person is creative, imaginative, and unorthodox. They are clever, innovative, creative, very intelligent, serious-minded, idea people, and good at tackling difficult problems.

Resource Investigator. This person is extrovert, enthusiastic, and exploratory. They communicate well, are consumed by curiosity, explore ideas generated by others, and duly report back.

Shaper. This person is dynamic, challenging, and outgoing. They are high strung, imposing, and self-confident.

Monitor-Evaluator. This person is serious, strategic, and discerning. They are sober, prudent, unemotional, have superb critical-thinking abilities, a high degree of intelligence, and the ability to analyze problems and evaluate suggestions.

Teamworker. This person is mild, perceptive, and accommodating. They are sensitive, socially oriented, popular, communicative, and supportive of other people; they ignore the strengths and weaknesses of others and possess good listening skills.

Implementer. This person is disciplined, reliable, and efficient. They are anxious, conscientious, orderly, and self-controlled; they display great strength of character and pay great attention to the smallest detail.

Completer. This person is painstaking, careful, and conscientious. They are dutiful, predictable, self-controlled, and disciplined; they tend to be realists and possess a great deal of common sense.

Specialist. This person is single-minded, a self-starter, and dedicated. They possess a specialty or are an expert in a very specific area.

Not All Is Rosy with Belbin's Theory

There have been several studies that have attempted to correlate Belbin's team roles on a statistical basis, without much success (e.g., Broucek & Randell, 1996; Senior, 1997; Senior, 1998). However, the issue of what constitutes success or high performance in real teams in real organizations, rather than artificially constituted management game-playing teams, is more complex.

Winning or losing can rarely be measured. It appears that it might be difficult to measure valid and reliable team-dependent outcome variables in any systematic way by testing team role theories in the context of real teams in real organizations. Spending time devising formulas that not only withstand statistical verification, but also are relatable to the real world might be a fool's errand. What is not worth debating is the continual and widespread use of the team role concept and the idea that a balanced team is a prerequisite for the success of teams. This is particularly the dilemma with small and large corporations, in-house trainers, and external consultants in their pursuit of helping teams improve their team performance. Matching team roles to each team member to achieve an appropriate balance on a team, however, continues to appear to be a fruitful approach.

Chapter 6
How to Match the Right People to the Right Team

First, Match Functional Competencies with Team Competencies

It is safe to say that after a decision has been made to use teams, everyone must buy into designing effective teams and buy out of the "Let's just put a team together to do that" mentality. The basic tenet of implementing a team system is to recognize that effectiveness depends on a positive contribution from all members of every team. Therefore, selection of the right team members that match the objective of each team becomes pivotal to designing successful teams.

Crucial to the performance of teams are the abilities and behaviors of individual team members. These abilities and behaviors surface in the roles that team members play. Building on the work of Belbin (2000), roles can be created in two ways. The first is in terms of *functional competency.* That is the role that a person brings to the team based on their professional expertise or job function within the organization. The second way a role is translated is the *team competency,* which is known as the role the individual performs within a team.

Functional competency, for instance as a marketing manager, scientist, research and development manager, or head of a department, represents the job capabilities employees can bring to the team. As stated earlier, people are often chosen to fill a specific functional competency that is needed on a team on the basis of their availability. Therefore, the *only* reason they are selected is because their functional competency fits the appropriate task(s) that the team has been assembled to perform, and they happen to be available when the team begins its work.

However, people's functional competency, though fitting to a team in terms of experience and expertise for the task at hand, might not necessarily help the team when it comes to the decision-making and implementation process. Functional competency might not help in matters such as the way different team members approach a problem or task, the way team members interact with each another, and their style of behavior in general.

In addition, individuals will not only bring the characteristics of their functional competency roles to their activities as members of teams, but will also take up one or more team competency roles. For instance, a person might be naturally imaginative—a good idea person. Another might be good at gathering information or leading the team.

PRACTICAL TIP 7

Identify realistic team competency roles using Keen's Team Competency Roles.©

As indicated earlier, team effectiveness is dependent upon the presence of, and balance among, specific types of team competency roles. The following team competency roles are more contemporary breakouts building on the research of many team role theorists, namely Belbin (1993 and 2000) as well as Rocine and Irwin (1994), Senior (1997), and Fisher (et al., 1998). These more relevant and realistic team roles are called Keen's Team Competency Roles. These new team competency roles are:

- **The Doers**
  - **Organizers**
  - **Analyzers**
- **The Problem Solvers**
  - **Mobilizers**
  - **Thinkers**
  - **Stimulators**
- **The People Persons**
  - **Harmonizers**
  - **Catalysts**

Although Keen's Team Competency Roles build off of Belbin's team roles they do not require the use of Belbin's relatively inaccessible interplace survey from the United Kingdom to verify them. These roles can be easily sorted out and identified for each member of a team by using the ubiquitous Myers-Briggs Type Indicator® that most people have taken and most companies have used in the United States. Application of both Keen's and Myers-Briggs' theories will be discussed in the subsequent section.

The Doer Roles: Organizers and Analyzers

The first key to making a team successful is to have team members who are willing to work. Having a room full of thinkers is stimulating but not very productive. The Doer roles are task-oriented, where the focus is on the team's purpose and making sure the job is done correctly and accurately. The task-oriented team competency roles are the team Organizer and the team Analyzer. People in these two team competency roles are considered to be the cement that holds the team together and ultimately they accept the responsibility to complete the final details to get the job done.

Organizers. The Organizers are a synthesis of Belbin's Implementer and Completer roles and have similar characteristics to those two roles. This person is process oriented, thorough, orderly, detail oriented, and painstakingly accurate. This type of person is quiet and serious about what needs to be done. They are practical, orderly, logical, and realistic. They are dutiful and like procedures, rules, and discipline. They focus on the how, stick to deadlines, and suggest processes. They like to see that everything is well organized, will pay great attention to the smallest detail, and are willing to take responsibility to make that happen. They are traditional in their beliefs and devoted to the team and the task at hand. They have a tendency to be too task oriented and sometimes are too rigid in their responses to team needs. Sometimes such an individual tends to lack flexibility and does not respond well to unproven, new ideas that do not fit the company's normal paradigms. They need to develop patience for those who do not follow standard operating procedures or who are not willing to accept the old, tried-and-true methodologies.

Analyzers. The Analyzers are modeled after Belbin's Monitor-Evaluator and have similar characteristics to that role. This person is logical, resourceful, factual, expedient, realistic, and expedient. This type of person is also quiet and reserved. They are usually interested in generating data. They make sure solutions are workable and sound because they look for cause and effect.

They have a tendency to be more adventurous and adaptable than an Organizer. They respond quickly when trouble arises and usually act as troubleshooters. They are prudent and unemotional individuals, thus have a calming effect on others when things do not go as planned. They use practical techniques to solve problems and are able to overcome obstacles in their way. They are project oriented. However, they sometimes lack follow-through if they do not see expedient results of their efforts. On their own, they appear to be indecisive and may be perceived as having low energy levels.

The Problem-Solver Roles: Mobilizers, Thinkers, and Stimulators

The next key to making a team successful is to have team members with the ability to create solutions. Having a room full of Doers might make the team organized, but not able to solve the problem on its own. The three Problem-solver roles are problem- and solution-oriented; the focus is on the team's objective and figuring out a way to get the job done. The problem- and solution-oriented team competency roles are Mobilizers, Thinkers, and Stimulators. People in these three team competency roles are considered to be the members that are able to solidify for others the problems that need to be addressed by the team.

Mobilizers. Mobilizers are modeled after Belbin's Resource Investigator and have similar characteristics to that role. This person is action oriented, outgoing, persuasive, resourceful, and extroverted. This type of person is friendly and drawn to fast-paced environments. They are usually able to solve problems using others as resources. They are very strong at developing and/or bringing resources from outside the experiences of the team to help solve problems. They make things happen by focusing on the immediate problem at hand and by taking the most expeditious route. They can usually find their way through difficult crises or issues. They have a network of resources to be able to find the right solution and are sensitive to the connections on the team and the outside resources. However, they need to work on project and time management techniques, rather than going for the immediate quick fix.

Thinkers.   Thinkers are modeled after Belbin's Plant and have similar characteristics to that role. This person is ingenious, analytical, conceptual, visionary, theoretical, imaginative, and introverted. This type of person is usually independent and individualistic, often preferring to work alone. They tend to be great at organizing ideas rather than situations or people. They are usually able to solve problems using cerebral resources. They are oriented toward the future and are the conceptualizers on the team. They have the ability to invent new things or view things from fresh, novel, and holistic perspectives. They make things happen by designing complex systems. They are usually good at solving intricate problems. They are not the most people-oriented members of a team and should not be looked to for acknowledgment or encouragement of others. They might at times complicate issues and use descriptions that confuse other team members.

Stimulators.   Stimulators are modeled after Belbin's Shaper and have similar characteristics to that role. This person is challenging, dynamic, driven, strategic, decisive, able to see the big picture, and goal-oriented. This type of person is usually conceptually oriented on the overall, long-term picture for the task. They tend to solve problems using logical reasoning, ingenuity, and unusual resources. They definitely gravitate to the more results-oriented projects because they tend to be take-charge individuals. That tendency will result in being the driving force on a team to complete the task or project. They become bored easily with mundane and routine projects and do not work well on those types of teams. Sometimes they do not factor in the human aspect of projects and need to validate the contributions of others.

The People Person Roles: Harmonizers and Catalysts

The next key to making a team successful is to have team members with the ability to hold the team together and make it function. Having a room full of Thinkers is exciting, but not if they do not recognize that other people exist. The two roles that are people-oriented, where the focus is on the team's objective and getting the job done using teamwork, are Harmonizers and Catalysts. People in these two team competency roles are considered to be the glue that holds the team together as people.

Harmonizers.   Harmonizers are modeled after Belbin's Teamworkers and have similar characteristics to that role. This person is caring, modest, reticent, cooperative, empathetic, loyal, and sensitive. This type of person is usually more concerned about others on the team than the project the team is working on. They are particularly sensitive to the concerns and feelings of others on the team. They tend to be compassionate, sensitive, and socially orientated people that harmonize the team by improving communications and generally enhancing team spirit. However, they may be too focused on others and attempt to please too many team members at once.

Catalysts.   Catalysts are modeled after Belbin's Coordinators and have similar characteristics to that role. This person is organized, appreciative, congenial, responsible, and tactful. This type of person is usually more concerned about gaining consensus on the team and how the team fits together as an entity or structure. They tend to be good listeners and able to negotiate with others on the team. He or she enjoys organizing and working with others on a variety of tasks, especially when the task is people oriented. They may tend to ignore their own needs. They do not appear to be overly creative problem solvers, but rely on the team to develop a solution, which they will then facilitate to closure. Unfortunately, they may have a tendency to be too process oriented towards accomplishing the goal and miss some of the nuances of the project or task.

PRACTICAL TIP 8

Identify each person's MBTI on a team.

This whole process works by taking the Myers-Briggs Type Indicator test. The test is available from many vendors for a fee. Make sure to obtain the test from an approved vendor who is certified to provide interpretation as well.

A modified version of the test is available for free simply by going to www.human metrics.com. Answer each question carefully and follow the instructions to view a description of your Myers-Briggs Type Indicator (MBTI®).

Katherine Briggs and her daughter developed the MBTI in the 1950s and produced a manual for decoding these type indicators. MBTI is known as a psychometric because it is a measurement tool. Apparently, MBTI is one of the most well-known and utilized personality model systems that exist today. Its derivative, the Keirsey-Bates Temperaments system, is closely aligned to the MBTI and available online. The author of this book tried both tests and was identified as the same type in each test. Although the author does not endorse either test, the previous statement is an example of whether the tests are comparable. Unlike Belbin's Interplace survey, MBTI has a long history of use and applicability in identifying people's basic personality types in the United States.

By linking a person's personality type as identified by the MBTI (or the Keirsey-Bates Temperaments test) and the required team competency for a particular team, a team's balance can be improved dramatically. Keen's Team Competency Roles can be applied easily to build a team once a person's MBTI has been established. The result is a well-balanced team!

The combination of Keen's Team Competency Roles and the MBTI will most likely result in the following matches:

Keen's Team Competency Roles	MBTI/Keirsey-Bates Types
The Doers	
• *Organizers*	ISTJ ISFJ
• *Analyzers*	ISTP
The Problem Solvers	
• *Mobilizers*	ESTP ESFP
• *Thinkers*	INFJ INTJ INTP
• *Stimulators*	ENTP ENTJ
The People Persons	
• *Harmonizers*	ISFP INFP
• *Catalysts*	ESTJ ESFJ ENFP ENFJ

PRACTICAL TIP 9

Balance the team membership based on the team mission.

To create a balanced team, identify the team mission and translate it into using the appropriate kind of team be it a Tactical, Operation, or Strategic team. A Tactical Team's mission usually centers on how to solve quickly a defined, immediate problem. Tactical Teams usually include members from only one department. For example, Tactical Teams could be effective to solve a manufacturing workflow problem. An Operation Team's mission usually centers on solving a problem that has broader implications on the organization's ability to function effectively and/or efficiently over the near term. Operation Teams usually include members from several cross-functioning departments whose combined expertise is relevant to a broad problem. For example, Operation Teams could be effective to evaluate and improve the organization's order processing procedure. A Strategic Team's mission usually centers on developing a company-wide approach that will define a new or long-term direction for the future of the organization. Strategic Teams usually include top-level managers representing key areas of the organization so the output is relevant for all areas of the organization. For example, Strategic Teams could be effective for developing the most appropriate organizational structure to fit its needs for the next 5- to 10-year planning horizon. Obviously, a Strategic Team's balance of team competencies will be significantly different than the balance of an Operation Team or a Tactical Team.

Matching Keen's Team Competency Roles and the MBTI for each kind of team might result in the following configurations:

	Tactical Team	Operation Team	Strategic Team
Doers			
Organizers	X	X	–
Analyzers	X	X	–
Problem Solvers			
Mobilizers	X	X	X
Thinkers	–	X	X
Stimulators	–	X	X
People Persons			
Harmonizers	–	X	–
Catalysts	X	X	X

Assuming a hypothetical membership of ten people per team, each kind of team might result in the following composition:

	Tactical Team	Operation Team	Strategic Team
Doers			
Organizers	3	1	–
Analyzers	3	1	–
Problem Solvers			
Mobilizers	2	2	1
Thinkers	–	1	5
Stimulators	–	1	3
People Persons			
Harmonizers	–	2	–
Catalysts	2	2	1

Balanced Teams = Successful Teams

By combining the Keen's Team Competency Roles, employees' MBTI, the mission of the team, and the appropriate kind of team, a team-structured organization can improve its team success rate. The alternative to this balanced method of team development is to use one of the ineffective team-development approaches outlined in a previous chapter. By balancing the team mission and kind of team with the appropriate membership based on functional competency roles and team competency roles, not only will the team members be more comfortable with their placement on the team, but they should be more successful, too!

Chapter 7
How to Cope with Team Issues

Learn to play by the rules.

According to Tompkins (1993), there are six rules to participating in a team environment.

1. Total honesty. Team members must feel like they can say what they think in team meetings. Every team member must feel comfortable expressing what they feel is part of the issue at hand and the ultimate solution.
2. Total amnesty. This author feels this is the most important rule. Team members must feel that whatever they say (positively or negatively) will not be held against them later on. For example, contentious language should not be included in the team minutes. Only information that members agree on as a unified group needs to be reported in the minutes of team meetings.
3. Listen. Team members must be willing to participate in active listening. If all members do not possess this skill set, team training could and should be focused on developing listening skills.
4. Focus. Team meetings must stay focused on the issues at hand. Active listening skills will help achieve this goal. Members need to concentrate only on the topic at hand and should discourage sidebar discussions among members. This focus will achieve results; the sidebars will just waste everyone's time.
5. Time management. Meetings should last only an hour or only as long as it takes to get the designated task done.
6. Come prepared. Tasks assigned at the last meeting must be considered a priority among all team members. Uncompleted tasks are only disrespectful of other team members' time and commitments.

In addition to these six rules identified by Tompkin, there is a seventh rule: play nice. The teams should enjoy meetings and have fun. Not to distract from the task at hand, but merely to reflect the proper balance between work and play.

Gaining Consensus

Any team's goal should be to reach decisions that best reflect the thinking of all team members. However, this does not always happen quickly on every issue. If the team gets bogged down in not reaching a decision, the Team Champion should attempt to make the team operate by what is called reaching consensus. Not every decision the team makes needs to have the support of every member. Most likely, it is impossible to have total agreement on every decision facing the team. Aiming for consensus at a team meeting requires a much different mind-set for each member than a traditional committee meeting. Gaining a unanimous vote for a committee can result in many arguments and discussions.

To reach consensus on a team, each member must participate fully in the development of a decision. This probably means also going through several rounds of discussions. Because the team is not seeking total agreement, the discussions have an end-point, that being consensus. The team will most likely know when it has reached consensus. This might be the point where not everyone is completely satisfied with the decision, but everyone can live with it.

It is easy to be confused about consensus, especially if the team is in a bureaucratic organization. Consensus is finding an outcome that everyone can support. Said another way, it is an outcome that no one opposes.

Consensus is not a unanimous vote, because it may not represent everyone's first selection. Consensus is not a majority vote, as this implies that there are members who agree and disagree with the vote. Therefore, consensus is not when all members are totally satisfied. However, everyone is satisfied enough that the team can move on to other decisions.

Gaining consensus is not easy. It requires time to gain everyone's input and concerns on issues. Therefore, time is needed at the team meetings to ensure the active participation of all members. Achieving consensus can also require team members, or the Team Champion at a minimum, to have some level of training on the elements of listening, conflict resolution, and discussion facilitation. Finally, gaining consensus requires creative thinking and open-mindedness among all of the members. This is sometimes the most difficult thing to achieve.

Team Training Issues

For teams to function properly, all team members should be trained to understand how to deal with the following operational issues:

Scheduling Considerations. The team must develop its own timetable and one that the entire team accepts and embraces. The timetable should be broken down by assignment or task. It should provide a clear view of the timetable required to complete each task or part of the project. Most importantly, it must include due dates and expected delivery points. The team can be trained in developing flowcharts of schedules through the use of tools such as classic PERT charts.

Resource Needs Assessment.   The team needs to be trained on how to evaluate resources. Training should focus on determining the various resource streams as a way of identifying the resources needed on the project. It is important that the team feel empowered to reach out to other teams internally or to outsource their needs. Emphasis on the financial, human, production, and research information needed for the team's assessment is key to train the members to evaluate all resource needs.

Control Function.   The team must be exposed to new areas of functional expertise with which they currently might not have any experience. For instance, training should cover budgeting of expenditures and available funding; formulating alternate or contingency plans to allow for changes that might occur on the project; and creating an internal team approval process for required changes to the team's funding, timing, or resource allocations.

Reporting of Progress.   The team members need to understand that, although they are empowered, they must also communicate their progress to the rest of the company. This is especially important for teams that have a specific section of an overall project that has its own timeline. Training should focus on writing typical project status reports and updated progress reports. The team also needs to be provided with a guideline and procedure for taking meeting minutes. Ideally, this procedure should have each member take a turn at writing minutes. Therefore, the routine of documenting the actions of the team can be shared by all members.

This will also help to give the team a sense of self-facilitation that must become the accepted way of team operation.

Coping with Common Problems Using Teams

Another area is how the team copes with several of the more common problems that plague new teams.

Getting Started.   Teams commonly have trouble starting a project. They might wonder how to begin the task or project. This is especially common for employees who have never been on a team before. The team might wonder what actions to take next, suffer through false starts, and flounder in its discussions.

These problems at the beginning of a project suggest that the team is unclear or overwhelmed by its task or that members are not yet comfortable enough with each other. Clearly, the Team Champion's role is to nurture, reassure, confirm the team's direction, and make sure everyone knows why they are on the team and the team's mission. However, the Team Champion's role is not to solve team members' problems.

Floundering.   Teams also might flounder during each stage of the project. For example, team members might sometimes resist moving from one phase in the project to the next. Team members might even delay or postpone decisions or conclusions from fear of presenting poor results.

Floundering when making decisions can indicate that the team's work is not the product of consensus or that some members feel uncomfortable with the group's conclusions. This "hung jury" situation can be a major problem.

Floundering after completing one phase of the project and before entering another phase could mean that the team does not have a clear plan. Floundering at the end of the project usually indicates that the team members have developed a bond and are reluctant to go their separate ways or that they like teamwork and are reluctant to return to their stations and work alone.

When a team hits a snag in output, members need to be sympathetic about not moving forward, but not allow others to stop working on the project. The team members might need to reenergize and motivate themselves to finish what they started.

Dealing with Problem Participants

Some members might garner a disproportionate amount of influence or "talk time" on the team, especially if that member is an expert or a senior employee. The member might use technical jargon that intimidates the rest of the team or they may discredit, discourage, or outright forbid discussions involving their turf. These members tend to drag out their inputs or interrupt others. Such behavior can turn off other team members as well as result in a loss of efficiency for the team as a whole.

Here again, the Team Champion needs to lead the team and encourage discussions that are structured on the team's key issues rather than sidebars and encourage a balance of discussion within the team. The Team Champion helps members agree on key points and clearly focuses on the problem members. The Team Champion also displays a clear instance of gatekeeping during discussions with the team and makes it clear to everyone that balance of input makes strong teams. If all else fails, the champion approaches the problem team member in private (never in front of the rest of the group), identifies the problem, and asks for their help and cooperation in finding a solution to correct the problem behavior.

Rush to Get It Done

Many teams feel too much pressure to perform. This can lead to a series of random, un-systematic efforts to "get the job done and get out of here." Teams must be encouraged at the beginning of their formation process to have the patience and time to get the task right. If this rushed attitude begins to form, remind the team members that quality takes time, their role is to create a quality product, and they should consider other options as solutions to the problem. A team member can even give other members directional input on the other options. The Team Champion then becomes like the judge who sends the jury back into deliberation one more time.

Lost in Space

Sometimes the team will stray from its appointed task with wide-ranging, unfocused discussions. Sometimes these digressions are innocent or even help to ease the tension for a team. However, when it happens a lot, there is a problem.

Making sure that the team adheres to some simple structural procedures might be all that is needed. For example, require a written agenda for each meeting. Require each team member to write topics appropriate for discussion on flip-chart pages and tape them on the wall. This makes sure that everyone gets heard and is focused on the task at hand. Lastly, some gentle prodding might be appropriate. Simply say: This team has had trouble sticking to its task. Is there something we need to know that is stopping you all from staying on course? Normally, the team members will get the message and work it out themselves.

> **PRACTICAL TIP 11**

Learn the art of persuasion—without arm twisting.

At times, members of the team might require some gentle persuasion from the Team Champion or other team members. When such persuasion is applied gently, usually there is not a need for other tactics. However, there are times when the Team Champion must be more aggressive in the persuasion tactics. Jay Conger has some suggestions for being persuasive that should become part of the basic training for every Team Champion and every team member. Conger (1998) suggests the following four steps for effective persuasion:

1. Establish Credibility. Credibility can come from two sources: expertise or relationship. Expertise credibility can come from others' perception that the person makes sound decisions or has some unique or exceptionally strong functional talents. Relationship credibility happens over time. When people feel that an individual listens, comprehends, and works in the best interest of the team and team members, then trust develops. In addition to trustworthiness, integrity, honesty, and fairness are also important factors—no easy skill set in today's very competitive environment.

2. Frame Goals for Common Ground. Effective persuaders are good at framing their positions to others in a positive way. Another important aspect of goal-framing is to know your audience. Senior managers think differently than plant workers. Framing comes from effectively thinking through viable arguments, points, and counterpoints; listening to identify the hot buttons of others; and presenting a thoughtful and cogent view of the issue.

3. Provide Compelling Evidence.   Once credibility is established and a common frame is identified, persuasion becomes a matter of presenting all the evidence effectively so the audience can understand it. The effective use of language is paramount to presenting anything, especially when trying to persuade others. Stories, data, examples, metaphors, and analogies are all strong uses of language to persuade others.

4. Connect Emotionally with the Audience.   Showing passion without showing too much passion is a powerful way to influence and persuade the audience. It is important that an adjustment be made in the tone and mannerisms utilized so that they are consistent with the time that the issue is being made. Sometimes banging on the table is appropriate, and sometimes a gentle whisper will be equally impactful. The key is to find the correct emotional match to persuade the audience.

Team Conflict or Feuding

Sometimes a team environment becomes a battlefield for certain members. This feuding can be limited to only a few (i.e., two) members with the others merely acting as spectators to the others' sporting match.

Two approaches to this situation are helpful. For instance, if there is a known problem between certain team members, try not to put them on the same sub-team. Such conflict distracts and derails the team. If the feuding happens during the team's activities, try to resolve the conflict with each individual, then with the combatants together away from the rest of the team. Most importantly, push the combatants to develop common ground for the common good of the team. Make sure they not only agree, but also come to some sort of mutual contract that will provide ground rules for managing their differences without disrupting the team.

> ### PRACTICAL TIP 12

Establish ground rules for conflict resolution.

If a conflict or issue has not reached a satisfactory conclusion, additional steps might need to be taken to resolve the conflict. Gulbranson (1998) has established some realistic and meaningful ways to deal with conflict resolutions.

Build Firewalls During the Team Formation Process.   Recognizing that conflicts will arise and identifying the process for dealing with them results in firewalls. This amounts to flushing out a potential difficulty before it arises. Therefore, setting this attitude of recognition and acceptance early in the teaming process can build positive results in the future.

Discuss the Issue for Resolution.   Verify the existence of the issue. Utilize a direct questioning technique to understand the magnitude and dimensions of the issue. If this results in weak or invalid response it is less likely to take time away from productive team activities if it is tabled for discussion at a later time.

Stay Focused on One Issue.   Discuss one issue at a time. Do not stray into other areas. If the discussion does raise another issue, the team should assign a separate time to that discussion.

Aggressive Silence Is Key.   Employ the technique of aggressive silence, so that each person must concentrate on listening to the viewpoint and input of others. No overtaking interruptions are to be tolerated. Otherwise the discussion quickly deteriorates into disjointed discussions.

Use Questioning, Not Challenges.   Questions should be used to gain a true understanding of other people's points of view rather than using intimidating challenges. Questioning also helps to examine all aspects around the situation or issues in conflict. This allows the team to dig in to the issues to gain further understanding or identify the singular issues that are the real basis for the conflict.

Communicate with Your Body.   Only send out positive signals by avoiding negative body language. Positive body language means having open, receptive posture and strong eye contact and talking directly to a person's face without the use of judgmental facial expressions.

Chapter 8
How to Monitor Team Success

Focus on the Output

An old business adage is fitting for this chapter. In order for members to evaluate the success of their teams, they need to evaluate their output. This means that teams need to have processes in place to help them determine the effectiveness of their team. The following chart sums up why this is relevant:

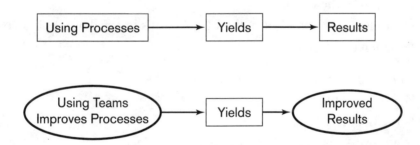

This section provides tools and approaches that team members can use to evaluate how their team is doing. They can choose the appropriate tool depending on the task and the team.

Oops!! It's Not Working?

What do you do if teams are not working? What happens if the new, flattened, empowered organization does not seem to respond? Consider a recent survey by Dumaine of *Fortune* 1,000 companies, which found that 68 percent of the organizations use self-managed or high-performance teams, but only 10 percent of the employees staff those teams. Based on this imbalance, it may be appropriate to conduct a reassessment of the situation and employee attitudes. Problems that might be uncovered and encountered while moving to empowered teams can range from the mundane and predictable to the more subtle.

To assess the situation, a macro and micro approach must be utilized. The situation must first be viewed from the perspective of the entire organization to determine if using teams has become a good fit with the operation of the firm. The macro evaluation looks at the situation through an internal audit in a holistic review of the firm. Secondly, a micro evaluation must occur with every team to ensure that the team process is functioning properly at the team level and for each individual on every team. A pre- and post-team audit conducted by each team should uncover any weak link(s) within the organization that might impair the success of the team approach. In addition, an audit of each team member's contribution to the team is required.

PRACTICAL TIP 13

Start with the big picture–dipstick the organization's team temperature.

Conduct an internal audit by answering questions listed in this section relative to how the team system fits into the overall operation of the company. Most importantly, the internal audit becomes one of the responsibilities of the Lead Team. It must be conducted on an impartial and unbiased basis. The goal is to conduct this internal audit of the relationship of teams to the overall functioning of the firm. It is imperative that the Lead Team be given not only autonomy to conduct this assessment, but it must also be given total and complete amnesty, in writing, from the CEO.

According to Keen and Keen (1998), the Lead Team's internal audit objective is to answer the following ten questions:

Question 1: Did top management do its job?
Question 2: Has enough time elapsed?
Question 3: Is the Lead Team a success?
Question 4: Is a process and a customer orientation in place?
Question 5: Is a new way of doing business evident?
Question 6: Are the goals clear and communicated effectively?
Question 7: Have tools such as benchmarking been used?
Question 8: Have the teams been trained effectively?
Question 9: Is teamwork evident?
Question 10: Do teams really feel empowered to manage themselves?

As an aid to assist in conducting the internal audit, a discussion of several facets of each question is provided.

Question 1: Did Top Management Do Its Job?

Once top management decided that teams were part of the future solution, did they contribute sufficiently to make teams work? Up front, top management is charged with several responsibilities, which include completely understanding how teams work, determining the impact of the change to using teams across the entire organization, and spending the time to make sure the organization was tooled-up for the transition to teams. As the ultimate communicators of the team approach, top management must provide a crystal-clear business reason for utilizing the team approach. The reason for being must be relevant so the teams can understand their role in the organization rationally. It must be communicated that teams are critical to helping the company achieve its goals and long-term health. If top management convenes teams so that fewer people could accomplish more work or as a financial strategy to show Wall Street a solution that deals with cost-reduction, human resources decisions, then it shows a lack of understanding of the team concept. Teams are not a simple solution or quick fix to business problems. They require a great deal of forethought and planning prior to implementation by top management.

In addition, top management must think through and develop a relevant vision for the teams to follow as a road map that provides an endpoint for the teams to aspire to in the company's new future state. Ideally, this vision is one that motivates each team member is worthy of personal embracement by each team member and is clearly, consistently, and constantly communicated to all team members. Also, top management must take a personal role in motivating the teams. This is required to project the change in image from an aloof management to an active, interested team management. If teams do not sense commitment and support from top management, a business as usual attitude can permeate and deteriorate the team effort.

Question 2: Has Enough Time Elapsed?

One of the key guidelines for utilizing teams from the guru of teams, W. Edwards Deming, is that they take time to work effectively. The transition from individual workers to teams takes time. A few, brief instructional meetings are not sufficient to make this transition. There needs to be time for all of the organizational, cultural, and personnel issues to sort themselves out.

The transition to teams is also very difficult. Effective teams take time to achieve the cohesion required to become top performers. According to management guru Peter Drucker, teams can take years to achieve a high level of competence. Time for conversion of the human factor within the organization also needs to be considered. In the old, hierarchical organization structure, individuals strove for individual success. In the team environment, individuals must relearn the concept of success as they strive for success of the team and the company. As a result, teams require constant nurturing of members and reassurance that the individual is important to the overall task at hand.

When the company exhibits a team culture, this is evidence that sufficient time has elapsed. This culture becomes evident, over time, once satisfying team experiences have occurred and significant success stories about team accomplishments appear throughout the organization. After these experiences and accomplishments are apparent, a team spirit should be evident. The teams should then exhibit more of a can-do attitude and confidence to operate independently.

Question 3: Is the Lead Team a Success?

As stated earlier, setting up a sub-team of cross-level and cross-functional employees is necessary to guide and nurture the team structure and operation. This Lead Team's responsibility is to maintain a top-level view of all of the team's activities to eliminate duplicity of activity. Lead Team members are also responsible for writing clear and explicit charters, which describe the specific deliverable for each team. As a result, they have the responsibility and authority to sanction the work and the establishment of a team.

More importantly, it is the Lead Team's role to provide reassurance to and instill trust in the organization that this approach can (or will) work. They must lead by example and be staunch advocates for the team process. They must be able to communicate their enthusiasm for the team system throughout everything they do, every day.

The most important contribution of this team, and for top management of the firm, is empowerment. The Lead Team must empower individual teams. The teams must feel that the empowerment is real and that top management will support their decisions. This trust level and delegation of power is sometimes difficult for top management to give up and out, but it is the key that unlocks the successful use of teams.

Question 4: Is a Process and a Customer Orientation In Place?

The firm must establish a process orientation for teams to follow. Widely available, easy-to-read charts tracking work, rework, schedules, etc., must abound in the organization. Only this process approach provides the internal mechanism for the team to become and stay self-managed. Other process tools, such as flowcharting every process, will be covered later in this chapter.

The firm must be customer oriented. Everyone, from the top to the bottom, must understand the customers' requirements in detail. This remains true for another perspective of exactly who the customers are for the firm. Customers are both inside (internal) and outside (external) the company. This means the orientation must include finding out what both internal and external customers want, need, value, and, most importantly, expect as the output of the teams. One way to accomplish this is to conduct internal and external customer surveys.

Question 5: Is a New Way of Doing Business Evident?

An entirely new system of reward and performance evaluation must be instituted and adhered to within the firm. This is critical for team members to take responsibility for managing and improving processes and changing the way they historically have viewed their jobs.

Everyone must recognize that the team approach to management is not the historical, customary way that employees have been doing their jobs. Employees must have positive guidance and assistance from the firm to make this transition from the old way to the new way. People will need support, feedback, and encouragement to help them learn this new way and make them feel comfortable and secure that everything will be all right. A transitional structure must be put in place to effect this change or the whole change process will take much longer and create enormous frustrations.

Question 6: Are the Goals Clear and Communicated Effectively?

Every team member needs a clear understanding of the endpoints for their team in terms of specific goals set forth for the project. The goals provide the boundaries that specific teams are chartered to accomplish. It is important that endpoints be in accord with the goals of the entire team, the team leader, and each team member. If not, members will be working towards goals for their own benefit, not the team's benefit. Any obstacles that stand in the way of the team meeting its goals must be identified as key issues to correct.

In addition, a sense of being able to articulate goals clearly is required. Specific goals must be established and, more importantly, communicated throughout the organization. These goals must reflect the current state of the firm, reflect what is needed as it moves into the transition state, and reflect the future state of the firm. The transition-state goals should be achievable and related to the changes that are required to move the company to the new culture. However, the future goals must be developed as stretch goals (goals that are not easily met) that will be more difficult to achieve.

Question 7: Have Tools Such As Benchmarking Been Used?

Have key analytical tools been effectively utilized as learning devices to facilitate the cultural change of using teams? One of those analytical tools is benchmarking, which will also be covered in detail later in this chapter. In order to be effective, analytical tools must be used in comparison to the best or most innovative internal departments, suppliers, or customers. Ideally, teams would benchmark against the company's best competitor(s) as it provides an actionable evaluation of what will be needed to compete more effectively. As a starting point, companies can benchmark well-known users of the team approach who have successfully adopted it and have changed their culture as a result. The main objective of benchmarking is to exploit what others have already developed and fit their approaches and innovations into the firm's operation. It is important to remember that benchmarking is not just a one-time event. To make any team extremely effective, benchmarking must become a way of life to continually improve team processes.

Question 8: Have the Teams Been Trained Effectively?

Proper training is critical to developing effective and productive teams. All team members must be trained to prepare themselves for this new way of work life. Also, it is important that each member have the ability to look for and feel empowered to have permission to bring up possible obstacles. Because there should not be any bosses on teams, everyone on the team must learn, and be willing to accept, unprecedented authority, responsibility, and decision making. Everyone must be trained in process improvement techniques, problem solving, interactive skills, and process methodologies such as flowcharting.

All team members must be trained in handling group conflict. In the old system, conflict was resolved by the person with the highest level of authority. On a team, group conflict, such as personality clashes, can point to the need for training to provide the entire team with the tools to deal effectively with conflict. Another training issue is the concept of consensus or compromise. Team members have to learn a mentality that suggests one can live with the team's decisions. Total agreement might not be achievable or even desirable among a team.

The team must be trained to seek solutions. Members must realize that they are in control and no one else is going to tell them what to do or how to do it. This shift in mental expectations is an important aspect to learn. The team must ask for and offer suggestions in a free and open environment. Therefore, the entire team will be comfortable evaluating suggestions openly and honestly.

Question 9: Is Teamwork Evident?

There are a number of key activities that result when there is effective team interaction. First, the team acts as a whole, not separate parts. All team members are open and honest with each other and willing to try new things. They must stretch themselves by thinking outside of their own boxes. They stay focused and do not deviate from their course of action. Unified team members do not belittle others on the team—either privately or publicly. The team enjoys what it is doing and has fun doing it.

The essentials of teamwork are also in place. These essential components of teamwork are:

- Everyone buys into the common goals of the team.
- A hierarchy of leadership within the team is elected by the team.
- All members are able to get along, interact well, and involve each other in team business.
- Open communication between all members is evident and no hidden agendas are tolerated.
- The team senses and acts with a feeling of empowerment.
- Everyone pays attention to both the process and the content of the team's activities.
- There is mutual trust among all members.
- There is respect for individual differences.
- The team employs constructive conflict resolution.

Basic tasks of teamwork are the functions required in selecting and carrying a group to completion of their goal. The tasks of teamwork are: initiating activity, getting information or opinions, giving information, and summarizing. Team members need to be initiating activity internally by proposing solutions and suggesting new ideas, new definitions of the problem, new attacks on the problem, or new organization of material. Teams need to seek information by asking themselves or other teams for their opinions or suggestions, as well as requesting clarification, additional information, or facts. Other important factors include cooperation and consensus, which are needed among all team members.

Conversely, teams need to be able to freely and openly give information by offering facts or generalizations, relating individuals' own experiences to the team problem to illustrate points, or by giving opinions concerning an outside or internal suggestion. Lastly, teams need to be able to summarize their tasks effectively by pulling together related ideas or suggestions and restating suggestions after the team has discussed them.

Question 10: Do Teams Really Feel Empowered to Manage Themselves?

The team must feel empowered to act and make decisions. One definition of empowerment is giving authority and enabling members to act on their own. This is the opposite of the bureaucratic hierarchical structure's concept of authority which means having layers of management with the power to force lower-level people to behave. Authority in an empowered organization means the individual or team has the power to get things done. Inherent to using empowerment successfully in a team environment is that competence comes from the ability of the team or team member to recognize problems and take action. Importantly, team members must not only feel comfortable with authority and power, but also be willing to take responsibility for their actions and the results of their actions.

Therefore, team members must understand that the old way, where authority meant power, is outdated. Under the team concept, power means everyone on the team has the ability to take action to get something accomplished. This concept of giving trust and empowerment to the employee has proven to be effective and operational according to E. Deming's work.

If this internal, corporate-wide audit is impartially completed by the Lead Team, the primary reasons for the inability of teams to perform effectively within the company should surface. Then the task becomes correcting the area(s) of deficiency. Depending on the findings of the audit, the correction could require a simple fix, such as providing more time for the transition, or a more complicated fix, such as reorganizing the entire structure of the company. However, going into the audit, top management must be willing to face the possibility that correcting the problems will be a more difficult task. They also must be willing to face the possibility that the problem might be top management.

Team Effectiveness Auditing Techniques

| PRACTICAL TIP 14 |

Complete a total team audit.

After the corporate view of the situation is obtained and appropriate corporate corrective action is put in place, the next area of examination is to review the performance of the individual teams through a microevaluation of each team. Thus, understanding the answers to the ten internal audit questions should identify the primary reasons for the inability of teams to perform effectively within an organization. To aid in the more actionable aspect of identifying why particular teams are not working, a total team development and internal audit form (Keen and Keen, 1998) has been prepared based on available literature and real business experiences using the team concept (see Figure 1). Although a number of tools and techniques exist for evaluating the entire team's performance, Figure 1 represents a total team audit form.

The rating scale requires a determination of either the team's satisfactory performance at one end of the scale, or unsatisfactory performance at the other. Teams with low numerical scores (a rating of five or less) on any element can immediately identify a problem area that needs attention.

TOTAL TEAM AUDIT

Team Name _____   Date _____

Competency	Team Needs Improvement									Team Excels
	1	2	3	4	5	6	7	8	9	10
The team understands corporate objectives.										
The team has translated corp. objectives into actionable team goals that everyone is committed to accomplishing.										
The team has completed all stages of the team formation process.										
The team operates effectively as a unit with everyone feeling part of the decision-making process.										
The team members recognize and appreciate individual differences and respect each other.										
The team proactively develops new ideas and solutions to achieve its goals.										
The team uses process tools to effectively accomplish tasks.										
The team has developed and adheres to defined timelines.										
The team maintains its focus and does not drift from its defined goals.										
The team acknowledges and effectively confronts internal conflicts.										

Figure 1   Total Team Audit
Source: Keen, Thomas R., 1997.

Each team member should anonymously but objectively fill out the form as an internal audit. It is important that each member give realistic ratings so that the team can identify its shortcomings. This provides a neutral ground for team members to highlight deficiencies within the team. A separate rating for the entire team should be calculated and compared to the benchmark for other teams.

In addition, the customers of each team should also fill out the form to provide a more complete view of the team's performance. The customer input should come from customers inside the company and customers outside the company. This separate score can also be compared with benchmark scores for other teams. A team that rates well on both measures can be comfortable about their team's performance. A team that has a high internal score and a low external score needs to have some serious discussions with its customers.

It is important that the audit be conducted at least twice as a benchmarking activity. The purpose of the first audit is to identify key weaknesses in the team and to evaluate the team's current state. A second audit should be conducted approximately six months after the first audit to determine if improvement has occurred. Thereafter, as continuous improvement should be a basic team objective, the audit can be used to guide the team through future activities.

PRACTICAL TIP 15

Complete a self-contribution audit.

One of the most effective monitoring devices to gauge team performance is to let the team members do it themselves. Human nature might drive the team members to be more critical and maybe more accurate. Given that situation, it can be very helpful for the team members to critically review their own performance on the team. The audit form in Figure 2 can help accomplish that review.

PRACTICAL TIP 16

Complete a peer audit.

There are a number of ways the team can evaluate team members' performance. Peer evaluations are excellent at uncovering a team's consensus that one member is not performing up to par. Through the peer evaluation forms, the deficient member can read objective comments about his or her performance. This avoids the problems of direct confrontation or a feeling of persecution by the member from other members of the team.

To complete the peer audit, consider evaluating each team member by answering some of the following questions:

■ Personal Characteristics
  • Are they warm and friendly?

SELF-CONTRIBUTION AUDIT			
Contribution	*Always*	*Often*	*Never*
1. I suggest new ideas, new approaches, or new courses of action.			
2. I suggest ways to organize the task at hand.			
3. I provide examples or illustrations for my ideas.			
4. I ask my teammates for information/opinions.			
5. I ask for clarification if I don't understand what others say.			
6. I like to suggest other people to contact or who can provide information on a subject.			
7. I attempt to bring the team back to the subject when the discussion goes too long.			
8. I get bored so I talk to others on the team during the meeting.			
9. I present reasons for my point-of-view.			
10. I see relationships between facts and the problem.			
11. I relate my comments to the contributions of others.			
12. I pull together and summarize ideas presented to the team.			
13. I encourage others to participate and present their ideas.			
14. I listen to the ideas and contributions of others.			
15. I support others when I think their ideas are good or important.			
16. I discuss the issues a lot during the meetings.			

Figure 2 Self-Contribution Audit
Source: Keen, Thomas R., 1997.

- Are they cooperative?
- Do they have a high tolerance for others?
- Do they have empathy for others?
- Are they sensitive to the needs of others?
■ Attendance and Preparation
- Do they attend every meeting?
- Are they punctual?
- Are they prepared for each meeting?
■ Commitment
- Are they committed to the team's purpose?

PEER MEMBER AUDIT

TEAM: _____   PROJECT:_____

Evaluate your performance first followed by your team members' performance. List team members in alphabetical order.

TEAM MEMBER   *PARTICIPATION**

1. Self:_____   _____ %*

    Evaluation: _____

    _____

    _____

2. Name:_____   _____ %*

    Evaluation: _____

    _____

    _____

3. Name:_____   _____ %*

    Evaluation: _____

    _____

    _____

                                                        Total must equal 100%

Figure 3   Peer Member Audit
Source: Keen, Thomas R., 1997.

- Are they results oriented?
- Do they display a strong personal commitment to ensure the team functions effectively?

■ Teamwork
- Are they a team player?
- Do they work well with all team members?
- Do they foster a climate of mutual respect?
- Do they recognize the contributions of others?
- Do they value the opinion of others?
- Do they help motivate other team members?

■ Problem Solving
- Do they stimulate others to solve problems?
- Do they think creatively (out of the box)?
- Do they get others to focus on the key issues?
- Do they help resolve conflicts?

■ Communication
- Do they convey open and honest communications?
- Do they demonstrate two-way communication?

- Do they demonstrate active listening?
- Can they influence others positively?
- Can they give meaningful feedback?
- Can they take constructive criticism to their ideas?
- Do they contribute with meaningful input?

The form in Figure 3 can be used as a peer audit form to evaluate each team member's contribution to the team.

Tools That Enable Teams to Achieve Effectiveness

Benchmarking

A key learning device and tool for facilitating the change into teams is benchmarking. Benchmarking must be done against the best or most innovative internal departments, suppliers, or organizations in other industries (or even competitors) to be effective. The main objective of benchmarking is to exploit what others have already developed and fit their approaches or innovations into the team's operation. Benchmarking is not just a one-time event; it must become a way of life to continually improve team processes.

The business orientation of benchmarking is the process of measuring performance against established norms from other companies or departments or against published industry statistics identifying successful team performance. Clearly, the goal of benchmarking is to move the team toward accomplishing its mission or charter. Benchmarking helps the team recognize superior performance; identify what is needed to improve effectiveness; and, most important for teams, determine areas of opportunity to improve.

The process of benchmarking involves several steps. First, identify the best of the best as a standard to which the team is compared. Second, identify areas of improvement and the goals needed to achieve success. This allows teams to develop the appropriate strategies to achieve those targets. Lastly, allow team members ownership of the plans required to achieve success. By doing this, this process provides the team the means to become the benchmark for other companies and achieve best-in-company or best-in-industry status.

Workflow Diagrams

Workflow diagrams (flowcharts) are used to break down an activity into identifiable parts. It is a step-by-step, schematic process used to understand a problem or to layout how the activity is currently being done. Through pictures of the sequence of events involved in an activity, the team members are provided with common, visual reference points and a standard view of the situation that they can use when talking about an existing process or project. These charts can be used as the tangible tool to visibly identify bottlenecks and problems to the current system. Importantly, teams can also use this tool to describe a desired sequence and order for a new, improved system. Flowcharts can be used to communicate to the rest of the organization the new process to be followed. They provide the visual representation that the other team members might need to understand the new way to operate.

Control Charts

Many factors affect a process over a period of time. A control chart is a time plot that lays out relevant data in chronological order. It can be used to plot a specific issue over a period of time. The period of time can be any length that is most appropriate for that particular issue.

Control charts also can be used to compare actual performance to a benchmark or to the target. Therefore, it shows variance against the benchmark or target over a particular period of time that can be used as the baseline to compare actual performance by the team.

Pareto Charts

A pareto chart is a series of bars whose heights reflect categories of data on a standard reference. The bars are arranged in descending order of height from left to right. This means that the categories represented by the tall bars on the left are relatively more important than those on the right of the chart.

Historically, most of the problems for a team are the result of a small number of issues or areas of poor performance. This tool is very helpful for teams to identify the real culprits of a problem. Teams can then focus their attention on the highest bars. This can be demonstrated by showing statistics versus other data (e.g., established norms) for key activities over a specific period in a chart format.

Chapter 9
How to Model Team Effectiveness

Start from the Beginning!

Use Keen's Team Effectiveness Model©.

The following team effectiveness model describes the ideal step-by-step process to achieve a successful result for the project or task at hand. (See Figure 4.)

Step 1: Identify Customer Needs and Concerns

No matter what the project, the first step is to identify the customer's desired output. The customer can be either internal or external. The output goal of any team has to be to exceed customer expectations, not merely to meet them. The goal of this step is to clearly understand the needs, concerns, and expectations of the customer. In doing so, the team can more easily clarify their reason for being and, therefore, the project goals.

Step 2: Design an Approach to Follow

The team's second task is to clearly design an approach to solve the problem or complete its assigned project. The team has a number of tools available to design the approach, a few of which are mentioned in chapter 8. Key during this step is to carefully lay out what information will be required to provide the input for the team to accomplish its goal. The team also needs to assign roles and responsibilities among the members for collecting and analyzing the data. Therefore, a plan can be developed that describes not only who will do what, but also a sequential timeline for completion of the aspects of the project.

Step 3: Collect Meaningful Data

Collecting meaningful data that will drive the team's activities becomes very important. Most teams are not made up of members with functional expertise. They normally have members with varying degrees of expertise that might not be relevant to the task at hand. Therefore, the team must go about collecting the right kind of data that will provide it with the input it needs.

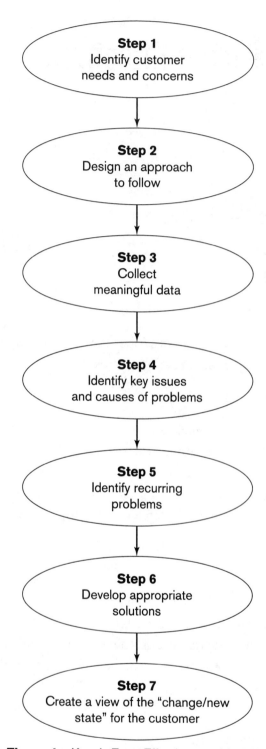

Figure 4 Keen's Team Effectiveness Model©

There are two key concerns during this step: developing operational definitions of the data so there is a common understanding among the team members and developing procedures and acceptable sources of the data so that consistency and stability for all collected data are achieved. Most importantly is what is called *right data.* This is data that is culled from existing sources for accuracy, relevance, and credibility. Right data has to be collected and sifted or cleaned for the team. Only the relevant data is needed. The "nice to know" data that might be interesting but not terribly relevant must be discarded before it is passed on to the rest of the team. This prevents the team from being side-tracked by irrelevant data. Finally, when collecting right data the most horrendous mistake must be avoided. All of the "wish to know" data must be kept from the team. This is data that will ultimately ruin a team by inundating them with totally irrelevant data that can completely distract the team from its primary goals.

Step 4: Identify Key Issues and Causes of Problems

Jumping to conclusions without understanding the real and major issues often leads the team down a path of wasted time and inefficient efforts. Localizing the occurrence of the key problems allows the team to focus and put its efforts on effectively identifying root causes of those problems. Some of the causes might be blatantly obvious to a team, especially if the team is not familiar with the issue. Normally, it takes more time and effort to develop the underpinnings of the problems. The team must complete a verifying process with existing data. This should help identify the actual causes of the problem and ensure that the correct data has been used to analyze and identify the correct cause of the problem. During this stage, any additional data that is needed to verify the team's conclusions will surface.

Most important to this step is a test of logic by all team members. Here the group dynamics of a team can be leveraged to ensure that all possible causes have been reviewed, eliminated, or abstracted from the data. This logic test will allow the team to re-review and fine-tune their conclusions before the team actually begins to solve the problem.

Step 5: Identify Recurring Problems

The team is now ready to categorize the problems it has identified. It is key to localize each major problem relative to its recurrence. The team must learn when and where these recurring problems exist. In other words, it must understand the trend for each problem. The more information that is developed, the better able the team will be to focus on the real source of these reoccurring problems. Localizing the problem directs a team toward the part of the problem that is the underpinning of what really needs improvement. If it only occurred once, it might be significant but not threaten the health and well-being of the customer. If it is recurring, a determination of why, when, and where this problem exists must consider codifying similar problems until the root of the problem surfaces. Therefore, these recurring problems can be attacked from a common base that can be applied to numerous situations, departments, or customers. Problems that are major but not continuously reoccurring can now be addressed by the team.

Step 6: Develop Appropriate Solutions

The charge of any team is to develop solutions that can really solve the problem. The only way for the team to really solve the problem is to identify the root causes of the problem itself. In order to do this, the team needs to take an objective look at the constraints, or unchangeable factors, that will limit the possible array of solutions. It might be that the most obvious answer is the best solution, but the team should always evaluate a range of alternatives to solve the problem. Key to this step is thinking outside of the box. The team needs to display creative problem solving and avoid the trap of finding the most acceptable but not the most effective solution. Clearly, by looking at the problem from a number of different angles, the team can open up to the possible solutions beyond the obvious ones.

The team can exhibit innovation and leadership by providing alternate as well as appropriate solutions to the customer. Therefore, it is important to develop a list of final candidate solutions to each major problem. The final list must consider things like practicality of implementation as well as resources of personnel, time, and money. A great solution might not fit with the customers' inherent capabilities and, therefore, not be a fit at all. Each final, alternative solution should be analyzed to identify possible weaknesses or shortcomings as well. Members should evaluate the amount of work and complexity of implementation involved in each alternative.

Next, compare the proposed final solutions and cull down to the most likely scenarios. These most likely solutions should be able to be implemented and communicated as simply as possible to the customer. Most importantly, the final solution must solve the root problem identified in step 4.

Step 7: Create a View of the "Change/New State" for the Customer

Unfortunately, most teams usually will not be part of the implementation process to execute their proposed best solution. However, the team has done all of the investigative reporting to develop the final solution, it has the best handle on what the result of the solution should be for the customer. Therefore, it is incumbent upon the team to identify for the customer a profile of what the customer should see after the proposed solution is in place. The team should provide their view of the changed state of the situation and what the situation should look like once the problem is solved. This last step is key for the team to have a sense of closure to its activity.

Now, Go Forth and Develop Successful Teams!

The *Merriam-Webster's Collegiate Dictionary,* 10th edition, defines *develop* as "going through a process." By combining all of the practical tips in this book into a process approach to utilizing teams, a team-structured organization can improve its success rate for developing teams. The alternative is to go back to the old approach of the 1900s of "let's put a team together to work on that" and hope for the best or accept the worst.

Bibliography

Al-Kazemi, Ali. (1998). The self-managed team and tori theory. *International Journal of Commerce & Management, 8,* 70–87.

Aubrey, C. A. (1988). *Teamwork.* New York: Quality Press.

Barry, D. (1991, Summer). Managing the bossless team: Lessons in distributed leadership. *Organizational Dynamics,* 31–47.

Barnard, Janet. (1998, Winter). What works in rewarding problem-solving teams? *Compensation & Benefits Management,* 55–58.

Belbin, R. Meredith. (1981). *Management teams: Why they succeed or fail.* Oxford: Butterworth-Heinemann.

Belbin, R. Meredith. (1993). *Team roles at work.* Oxford: Butterworth-Heinemann.

Belbin, R. Meredith. (2000). *Beyond the team.* Oxford: Butterworth-Heinemann.

Bennis, W., & Nanus, B. (1985). *Leaders: The strategies for taking charge.* New York: Harper & Row.

Bennis, W. (1991, August). Creative leadership. *Executive Excellence,* 5–6.

Bishop, Suzanne K. (1999, September). Cross-functional project teams in functionally aligned organizations. *Project Management Journal, 30,* 6–12.

Blanchard, K. (2000). *The one minute manager builds high performing teams.* Boston: Quill.

Block, P. (1987). *The empowered manager.* San Francisco: Jossey-Bass.

Braham, J. (1993, December 10). Building a winning team. *Machine Design,* 17.

Briggs-Myers, I., & McCaulley, M. H. (1985). *Manual: A guide to the development and use of the Myers-Briggs Type Indicator.* Palo Alto, CA: Consulting Psychologists Press.

Broucek, Willard G., & Randell, Gerry. (1996, December). An assessment of the construct validity of the Belbin Self-Perception Inventory and Observer's Assessment from the perspective of the five-factor model. *Journal of Occupational and Organizational Psychology, 69,* 389–405.

Burns, J. M. (1968). *Leadership.* New York: Harper & Row.

Capezio, Peter. (1998). *Winning teams: Make your team productive & successful.* Franklin Lakes, NJ: National Press Publications.

Carnegie, D. (1993). *The leader in you.* New York: Simon & Schuster.

Caudron, S. (1994, October). Tie individual pay to team success. *Personal Journal, 73,* 40–46.

Chadwell, T. (1993, March 13). Self-direction: A hot topic. *The Business Journal, 15,* 102.

Chang, Richard Y. (1994). *Building a dynamic team: A practical guide to maximizing team performance.* San Francisco: Jossey-Bass.

Chang, Richard Y., & Curtin, Mark J. (1994). *Succeeding as a self-managed team: A practical guide to operating a self-managed work team.* Chang Association.

Cohen, W. H., & Cohen, N. (1984). *Top executive performance.* New York: John Wiley & Sons.

Component, Paul J., & Farrington, Phillip A. (2000, March). Identification of effective program-solving tools to support continuous process improvement teams. *Engineering Management Journal, 12,* 23–29.

Conger, Jay A. (1998, May/June). The necessary art of persuasion. *Harvard Business Review,* 84–95.

Convey, Steven. (1994, October). Performance measurement in cross-functional teams. *CMA,* 13.

Davis, K. (1967). *Human relations at work.* New York: McGraw-Hill.

Davis, J., Millburn, P., Murphy, T., & Woodhouse, M. (1992). *Successful team building: How to create teams that really work.* London: Kogan Page.

Deming, W. E. (1986). *Out of the crisis.* Cambridge, MA: Massachusetts Institute of Technology, Center for Advanced Engineering Study.

Donnellon, Anne. (1996). *Team talk.* Boston: Harvard Business School Press.

Donnelly, R. G., & Kezsbom, D. S. (1994, May). Overcoming the responsibility-authority gap: An investigation of effective project team leadership for a new decade. *Cost Engineering,* 33–41.

Drucker, P. F. (1980). *Managing in turbulent times.* New York: Harper & Row.

Dumaine, B. (1994, September 5). The trouble with teams. *Fortune,* 86.

Engleberg, Isa, & Wynn, Dianna. (2000). *Working in Groups.* New York: Houghton Mifflin.

Eisenhardt, Kathleen M. (1999, Spring). Strategy as strategic decision making. *Sloan Management Review,* 65–78.

Felts, Cathy. (1995, March/April). Taking the mystery out of self-directed work teams. *Industrial Management,* 21.

Fisher, S. G., Hunter, T. A., & Macrosson, W. D. K. (1998, September). The structure of Belbin's team roles. *The Journal of Occupational and Organizational Psychology, 71,* 283–288.

Flores, F. P. (1992, April). Team building and leadership. *Supervisory Management,* 8.

Fowler, Alan. (1995, February 23). How to build effective teams. *People Management,* 15–19.

Gooley, T. B. (1993, September). Team spirit. *Traffic Management,* 67–68.

Green, Fess B., & Henderson, Dale A. (2000, March/April). Tools@work: Nine ways to evaluate the effectiveness of your team-based organization. *The Journal for Quality and Participation, 23,* 36–39.

Gregory, Annie. (1999, January). Solving the teambuilding jigsaw. *Works Management,* 56–59.

Gross, Steven E. (1997, January/February). When jobs become team roles, what do you pay for? *Compensation and Benefits Review,* 48–51.

Gulbranson, Jeanne E. (1998, May/June). The ground rules of conflict resolution. *Industrial Management,* 4–7.

Gustafson, K., & Kleiner, B. H. (1994). New development in team building. *Industrial & Commercial Training,* 17–22.

Hallam, Glenn L. (1996). *The adventures of team fantastic: A practical guide for team leaders and members.* Center for Creative Leadership.

Harrington, H. J. (1995). *Total improvement management: The next generation in performance improvement.* New York: McGraw-Hill.

Harrington-Mackin, Deborah. (1995, April). Twelve ways to facilitate meetings. *Supervisory Management,* 8.

Harrington-MacKin, Deborah. (1993). *The team building tool kit: Tips, tactics, and rules for effective workplace teams.* New York: Amacom.

Harris, Richard C., & Lambert, Jean Trescott. (1998, September/October). Building effective R&D teams: The senior manager's role. *Research Technology Management,* 28–35.

Hersey, P., & Blanchard, K. H. (1982). *Management of organizational behavior: Utilizing human resources* (4th ed.). Englewood Cliffs, NJ: Prentice Hall.

Hickman, Gill Robinson, & Creighton-Zollar, Ann. (1998, Summer). Diverse self-directed work teams: Developing strategic initiatives for 21st century organizations. *Public Personnel Management,* 187–200.

Hirsh, Sandra. (1985). *Using the Myers-Briggs Type Indicator in Organizations.* Palo Alto, CA: Consulting Psychologists Press.

Hirsh, Sandra, & Kummerow, Jean. (1998). *Introduction to type in organizations.* Palo Alto, CA: Consulting Psychologists Press.

Hitchcock, N. A. (1993, February). Can self-managed teams boost your bottom line? *Modern Materials Handling,* 47.

Huber, G. P. (1980). *Managerial decision making.* Oakland, CA: Scott Foresman & Co.

Johnson, Robal. (1996, April). Effective team building. *HR Focus,* 18.

Johnson, S. T. (1993, March/April). What's ahead in work design and rewards management. *Personnel Journal, 61,* 46.

Joinson, Carla. (1999, May). Teams at work. *HR Magazine,* 30–36.

Katzenbach, J. R. & D. K. Smith. (1993). *The wisdom of teams.* New York: Harper Collins.

Katzenbach, Jon R. (1997, November/December). The myth of the top management team. *Harvard Business Review,* 82–91.

Keen, Thomas. (1998, February). Self-managed teams: Is this approach working? *APICS—The Performance Advantage,* 46–48.

Keen, Thomas, & Keen, Cherie. (1998, February). So the team approach isn't working—Now what do you do? *Training & Development,* 13–15.

King, D. (1998). *New patterns of management.* New York: McGraw-Hill.

Kirkman, Bradley L., & Rosen, Benson. (2000, Winter). Powering up teams. *Organizational Dynamics,* 48.

Koller, A. (1989, November/December). Developing and managing a winning steam. *Manage,* 2–9.

Kotter, J. P. (1988). *The leadership factor.* New York: The Free Press.

Launchbury, Keith J., & Bloom, Claire V. (1999, August). Effective evaluation of team performance. *Hospital Material Management Quarterly,* 48–52.

Lyman, Dilworth, & Richter, Ken. (1995, February). QFD and personality type: The key to team energy and effectiveness. *Industrial Engineering,* 57.

Litsikas, Mary. (1995, September). Overcome team problems. *Quality,* 26.

Martin, D. (1993). *Team think: Using the sports connection to develop, motivate, and manage a winning business team.* New York: Penguin Books.

McChesney, Harvey III. (1995, May). The facilitator: As teams battle to be effective. *Hospital Material Management Quarterly,* 6.

McIntyre, Marie G. (1999, July/August). Five ways to turn your management team into a leadership team. *The Journal for Quality and Participation, 22,* 40–44.

Mohrman, Susan Albers, Mohrman, Allan M., & Mohrman, Allan M., Jr. (1997). *Designing and leading team-based organizations: A workbook for organizational self-design.* San Francisco: Jossey-Bass.

Moody, Maureen. (1999, January). Father of the team. *Director,* 72.

Moxnes, Paul. (1999, November). Deep roles: Twelve primordial roles of mind and organization. *Human Relations,* 1427–1444.

Naisbitt, J., & Aburdene, P. (1991, March). New leadership. *Executive Excellence,* 10–12.

Panchak, Patricia. (1998, September 21). The future of manufacturing: An exclusive interview with Peter Drucker. *Industry Week,* 86–87.

Parker, G. M. (1990). *Team players and teamwork: The new competitive business strategy.* Oxford: Jossey-Bass.

Pell, Arthur R., & Ashby, Franklin C. (1999). *The complete idiot's guide to team-building.* London: Macmillan.

Perry, Ian. (1997, July). Creating and empowering effective work teams. *Management Services,* 8–11.

Rocine, Victor, & Irwin, Don. (1994, October). Make team members responsible for team effectiveness. *CMA,* 28.

Schermerhom, J. R., Hunt, J. G., & Osborn, R. N. (1994). *Organizational Behavior.* New York: John Wiley.

Schwartz, A. E., & Catalano, C. (1991, May/June). How the new leaders will manage in the 1990s. *Nonprofit World,* 22–24.

Senior, Barbara. (1997, September). Team roles and team performance: Is there really a link? *Journal of Occupational and Organizational Psychology, 70,* 241–258.

Senior, Barbara. (1998). An empirically based assessment of Belbin's team roles. *Human Resource Management Journal, 8,* 54–60.

Shaw, T. (1976). *Group Dynamics: The psychology of small group behavior.* New York: McGraw-Hill.

Shaw, Douglas G., & Schneier, Craig Eric. (1995). Team measurement and rewards: How some companies are getting it right. *Human Resource Planning, 34.*

Smith, Richard. (1993, October). What a team! *Management Accounting, 71* (9), 48.

Spaulding, M. (1994, February). Worker teams go avant garde. *Packaging, 92.*

Szilagyi, A. D., & Wallace, M. J. (1990). *Organizational behavior & performance.* New York: Harper Collins.

Tompkins, James A. (1993, April). Team-based continuous improvement. *Material Handling Engineering, 47.*

Tolle, E. (1988, January). Management team building. *Engineering Management International,* 277–285.

Townsend, Anthony M., DeMarie, Samuel M., & Hendrickson, Anthony R. (1996, September). Are you ready for virtual teams? *HR Magazine, 122.*

Trimble, Susan, & Walker, John W. (1996, December). Creating, invigorating, and sustaining effective teams. *NASSP Bulletin, 35–40.*

Tuckman, B. W. (1965, Number 63). Developmental sequence in small groups. *Psychological Bulletin, 384–399.*

Uhlfelder, H. F. (1994, July/August). Leadership + teamwork + commitment = success. *Journal for Quality & Participation, 17,* 24–27.

Verespeg, Mike. (1998, April 6). Drucker sours on teams. *Industry Week, 102–05.*

Weinstein, S. (1992, September). Teams without managers. *Progressive Grocer, 87.*

Wellins, R. S. (1992, December). Building a self-directed work team. *Training and Development, 12–14.*

Wellins, S., Sr., W. C. Byham, & J. M. Wilson. (1992). *Empowered teams.* San Francisco: Jossey-Bass.

White, Jim. (1999, September). Teaming with talent. *Management Today, 56–61.*

Willcocks, Graham, & Mosrris, Steve. (1997). Successful team building. *Barrons.*

Woods, John A. (1997). *10 minute guide to teams and teamwork.* Alpha Books.

Zemke, Ron. (1992, April). Second thoughts about the MBTI. *Training, 43.*

Zenger, J. H., Wusselwhits, E., Hurson, K., & Perrin, C. (1992, September). Managing: Leadership in a team environment. *Security Management, 28–33.*

Index